BEARTOOTH COUNTRY

Montana's Absaroka and Beartooth Mountains

GEORGE WUERTHNER PHOTO

BY **BOB ANDERSON**

MONTANA GEOGRAPHIC SERIES / No SEVEN; REVISED EDITION

MONTANA MAGAZINE/AMERICAN & WORLD GEOGRAPHIC PUBLISHING

MICHAEL S. SAMPLE

JOHN REDDY

Library of Congress Cataloging-in-Publication Data
Anderson, Bob
    Beartooth country : Montana's Absaroka and Beartooth mountains
/ by Bob Anderson. -- Rev. ed.
        p.   cm. -- (Montana geographic series : no. 7)
    ISBN 1-56037-065-3
    1. Natural history--Beartooth Mountains (Mont. and Wyo.) 2.
Natural history--Absaroka Range (Mont. and Wyo.) 3. Absaroka
Range (Mont. and Wyo.) Beartooth Mountains (Mont. and Wyo.)
    I. Title. II. Series.
    QH104.5.B42A53 1994
    978.66--dc20   94-30004

Write for our catalog:
American & World Geographic Publishing, P.O. Box 5630,
Helena, MT 59604.
Printed in U.S.A. by Fenske Companies, Billings, Montana.

Above: *Aerial view of alpenglow on Granite Peak.*
Right: *Indian paintbrush.*
Facing page, left: *Winter on Mount Zimmer, above Goose Lake.*
Facing page, right: *Lupine blooms in the East Boulder River Valley.*

Title page: *Upper Mill Creek below Crow Mountain.*

Front cover: *Ice on unnamed lake by Lonesome Mountain.* GEORGE WUERTHNER
Back cover, left: *Yellow balsamroot and purple lupine.* LARRY JAVORSKY
Back cover, right: *East face of Mount Cowen.* BOB ANDERSON

CONTENTS

ACKNOWLEDGMENTS

The first edition of this book was the product of the efforts of many people who unselfishly shared their time, their encouragement, their wisdom, their knowledge, and their advice. None, however, would accept responsibility for even the slightest error in the text. Those remain the burden of the author.

One of my best sources of information was Judd Moore, the information officer for Region One of the Forest Service. Judd was always cheerful, prompt, responsive, and helpful.

When I started this project I had never seriously studied history; I viewed the recent past as a necessary but uninteresting aspect of the book. That attitude was short-lived. Much to my surprise and delight, the history of the region became my passion. Dave Walter of the Montana Historical Society made it painless with his always prompt and accurate assistance. Among the others who planted and fertilized the historical seeds were Aubrey Haines, Bill Lang, Doris Whithorn, Dennis Lutz, Ralph Glidden, and Minnie Paugh. The treatment of the Beartooth's history presented here is by no means complete, but, with the help of these people, I have uncovered interesting stories.

Some of the historical research led to clear but negative answers. For example, Frederick Renner and Malcom McKay assured me that Charles M. Russell had never visited the Beartooth or Cooke City as had previously been written. Nor was Lillian Gish ever associated with the Gish Mine on the Boulder River. Her gracious letter, however, made me a devoted fan of hers. Her death in 1993 was mourned by the world.

Among the non-historians who were of immeasurable assistance with historical facts were Ruth Koch, Frieda Urey, and Cornelius Bliss.

The description of Anders Wilse's 1898 trek to the Beartooth was cheerfully translated from the Norwegian by David Fluharty.

The most exciting part of the book is the list of alpine plants, appended to the back of the volume. Such a list has never been published for the entire Beartooth, and the list for no other alpine area in the world is as long. I am especially grateful to Klaus Lackschewitz, the dean of Montana alpine botany, for compiling the list and for meticulously proofreading it several times. The wildflowers, in particular the alpine ones, are extremely personal to me and I am eternally grateful to Klaus for increasing both my knowledge and my appreciation of them. Also helpful with alpine botany were Peter Lesica and Jerry Moore.

Tom Koch of Hamilton, grandson of Peter Koch and son of Elers Koch, generously shared the Anders Wilse prints of the Beartooth and the photos of the first ascent of Granite Peak. Lory Morrow, photo archivist at the Montana Historical Society, was also extremely helpful.

I owe a debt of enduring gratitude to my friend

Bob Decker, who shared some fine Beartooth moments with me and improved the text beyond recognition by suggesting many ways to add life and interest to this engineer's prose.

This revised edition was possible only with the assistance of researcher Phyllis LeFohn, always cheerful, indefatigable, efficient, thorough and inquisitive. Her investigations enabled me to avoid being swallowed up by the curiosity research stimulates, and to meet my deadline. She got prompt and constructive responses from: Heidi and Jim Barrett, Bob Clark, Mike DaSilva, Bob Dennee, Carol Ferguson, Bonnie Heidel, Mary Lennon, Blase DiLulo, Lil Erickson, Bruce Gilbert, Amy Grubs, Lyle Hancock, Mark Henckel, Randy Herzberg, Greg Jahn, Michael Kakuk, Ted Lange, Steve Morton, Richard Parks, Pat Pierson, John Pinegar, Rick Ryan, Kimberly Schlenker, George Shaller, Brian Shovers, Ray and Trudy Shunk, Sherm Sollid, Darlene Staffeldt, Richard Stiff, Andrea Stander, Vicki Terbovich, Jeannie Thompson, Bea Vogel, Hugh Zackheim, and many others.

Sadly, by 1994, Klaus Lackschewitz was in failing health. Nevertheless he was able to add several species to his 1984 list of alpine plants. Peter Lesica added species he collected on the Line Creek Plateau and also critically reviewed the text.

Some of the oldest rocks on planet have been found in the Beartooth Mountains, many by Dave Mogk who shared his knowledge and provided a contemporary interpretation of the Archean geology.

Other extremely helpful sources for the revised edition included: Sandra Cahill, Bob Crabtree, Charlie Eustace, Jack Fanshawe, David Gallaird, Paul Hendricks, Bonnie Heidel, John Hoak, Dick Johnson, Dick Knight, Bart Kohler, Cary Lund, Bob Moore, Harold Picton, Mike Poore, Steve Shelly, Jeane-Marie Souvigney, Shawn Stewart, and Nathan Varley.

Finally, my undying gratitude to Linda, for her steadfast support and a long leash.

Below: Near Goose Lake.

Facing page: Mary Lake.

RICK GRAETZ

PREFACE

As I was growing up in Livingston, my backyard was the Absaroka Mountains south of town. Like most kids in that railroading community, my first exposure to the mountains was the Pine Creek Campground, known locally as Luccock Park. From there, my exploration urges took me to Pine Creek Falls and, finally, the lake.

Pine Creek is, and has been for decades, one of the most heavily visited drainages in the Absaroka-Beartooth. But outside its steep confines lies some of the wildest, most rugged country in Montana. From the beginning, I longed to know what mysteries the high ridges hid from me.

As I grew older, I ventured farther. To Elbow Lake. To Emigrant Peak. To Davis Creek. Each sortie gave me immeasurable joy, and the vastness of the wilderness increased my need to explore.

Naturally I took my backyard for granted. Beyond the fence, where the grass was greener, lay the Beartooth. On the wall beside my bed I mounted the Cooke City and Alpine U.S. Geological Survey maps. Night after night I reveled in my awe of the lakes, the glaciers, the endless, treeless plateau, the peaks, and the streams. It was Nirvana…Utopia.

My introduction to what I understood was the Beartooth came by way of the Boulder River. Luther Lodge, the Bible camp farthest up the canyon, lay on the union of the Mount Cowen and Mount Douglas quadrangles. Both east and west, up Upsidedown and Bridge creeks, my friends and I explored. Each year we got bolder. Finally, by the time I was in high school, we could agonize through a morning of required Christianity, bolt

Yellowstone River in the Paradise Valley.

our lunches, then streak up the trail to Horseshoe Lake, to Rainbow Lakes, to Bridge Lake, or to the Hellroaring divide. The return trip, often at a full gallop, usually beat the dinner bell.

Camp officials frowned on these unsupervised treks, but in vain. Sooner stop a freight train. The drive to explore the alpine was irrepressible.

From the heights—Emigrant Peak, Haystack Peak, Mount Baldy—we could often see Pilot and Index peaks, faint, tiny, but unmistakable on the hazy horizon. Not only were they striking landmarks, but they symbolized the vastness of the Beartooth.

Forty years later, my lust for exploring the Beartooth has yet to subside. Oh, sometimes I worry that I might someday go everywhere and

lose the intrigue of the unknown. But after each trip I return with a wish list of secret places to visit next year. The ultimate solitude. The unscaled exposures. The undiscovered lake with lunkers with my name on them. The endless summer.

I've learned that both the Beartooth and Absaroka ranges are larger than I thought as a child. That the Beartooth Mountains include the mountains south of Livingston called the Absarokas by local folks. That the Absaroka Range technically includes the Beartooth Range and extends well into Wyoming. But these semantic technicalities have no relevance. What is important is that the mountains of my youth—the Absaroka-Beartooth—are the center of the universe.

The Beartooth Range Land Ownership

Map by Ed Madej

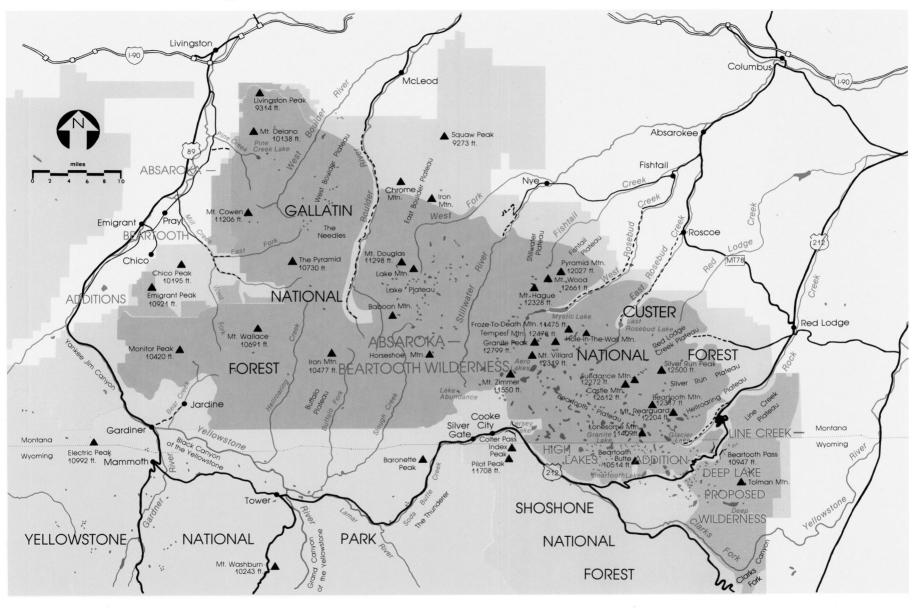

N

miles
0 2 4 6 8 10

I-90 Livingston

McLeod

Columbus

I-90

89

ABSAROKA —

▲ Livingston Peak 9314 ft.

Boulder River

Pine Creek

Pine Creek Lake

▲ Mt. Delano 10138 ft.

West Boulder Plateau

▲ Squaw Peak 9273 ft.

Absarokee

Fishtail

GALLATIN

▲ Chrome Mtn.

East Boulder Plateau

▲ Iron Mtn.

West Fork

Nye

Stillwater Plateau

Fishtail Creek

Fishtail Plateau

Roscoe

Creek

Rosebud Creek

212

MT78

Emigrant Pray

▲ Mt. Cowen 11206 ft.

The Needles

West

Creek

BEARTOOTH

Chico

Mill Creek

East Fork

NATIONAL

▲ The Pyramid 10730 ft.

Mt. Douglas 11298 ft. ▲

Lake Mtn. ▲

Lake Plateau

Pyramid Mtn. 12027 ft. ▲

▲ Mt. Wood 12661 ft.

Red Lodge Creek Plateau

CUSTER

Red Lodge

▲ Chico Peak 10195 ft.

ADDITIONS

▲ Emigrant Peak 10921 ft.

West Fork

▲ Baboon Mtn.

Mt. Hague 12328 ft. ▲

Mystic Lake

East Rosebud Lake

Red Rosebud Creek

NATIONAL

FOREST

▲ Mt. Wallace 10691 ft.

Helroaring Creek

▲ Monitor Peak 10420 ft.

ABSAROKA —

BEARTOOTH WILDERNESS

Froze-To-Death Mtn. 11475 ft.
Tempest Mtn. 12478 ft.
Granite Peak 12799 ft. ▲

Hole-In-The-Wall Mtn. ▲

▲ Mt. Villard 12349 ft.

Silver Run Peak ▲ 12500 ft.

Silver Run Plateau

Helroaring Plateau

FOREST

Yankee Jim Canyon

▲ Iron Mtn. 10477 ft.

Buffalo Plateau

▲ Horseshoe Mtn. ▲

Stillwater River

Aero Lakes

Sundance Mtn. 12272 ft.

Castle Mtn. 12612 ft. ▲

Beartooth Plateau

Mt. Rearguard 12204 ft. ▲

▲ 12347 ft

Line Creek Plateau

Jardine

Bear Creek

Buffalo Fork

Slough Creek

▲ Mt. Zimmer 11550 ft.

Lake Abundance

Cooke City

Kersey Lake

Glacier Lakes

LINE CREEK —

Montana

Wyoming

Gardiner

Black Canyon of the Yellowstone

Yellowstone River

Silver Gate

Lonesome Mtn. 11409 ft ▲

Granite Lake

Glacier Lake

Rock Creek

Montana
Wyoming

Electric Peak 10992 ft. ▲

Mammoth

Gardner River

Colter Pass
Index Peak ▲

HIGH

Beartooth Butte ▲ 10514 ft.

ADDITION

LAKES

Beartooth Lake

Beartooth Pass 10947 ft.

DEEP LAKE

▲ Baronette Peak

▲ Pilot Peak 11708 ft.

212

SHOSHONE

▲ Tolman Mtn.

PROPOSED

YELLOWSTONE

NATIONAL

Tower

Lamar River

Soda Butte Creek

The Thunderer

NATIONAL

WILDERNESS

Deep Lake

PARK

Grand Canyon of the Yellowstone

▲ Mt. Washburn 10243 ft.

FOREST

Clarks Fork

Clarks Fork Canyon

Yellowstone River

National Forest	National Park	Private Land	Designated Wilderness Areas	Proposed Wilderness Areas

INTRODUCTION

The name Beartooth evokes strong images of the rugged canyons and alpine plateaus of the land mass forming the headwaters of several drainages: the Clarks Fork of the Yellowstone, the Stillwater River, East and West Rosebud creeks, and Rock Creek. A neighboring region, from Livingston south to Mill Creek and extending eastward across Lake Plateau, is part of the Beartooth. But it is also called the Absaroka, and, by some, the Snowy (or Snow) Mountains. Over a century ago, it was called the Yellowstone Range.

Current geographical nomenclature uses the name Absaroka to refer to the range of mountains that extends from Livingston south and eastward to the eastern crest of Yellowstone National Park, nearly to Dubois, Wyoming, due east of Jackson Hole.

Absaroka is well known to be a Crow Indian name, often translated to mean "sharptailed bird," the name the Crows gave themselves. Robert Lowie, a prominent cultural anthropologist who studied Plains Indians in the early part of this century, subscribed to this view. Other definitions have been reported, among them: "the bird people," "descendants of children of the raven," "children of the large-beaked bird," "people of the sharptailed bird," and even "anything that flies."

Absaroka has labeled many things in addition to the mountain range. The Absaroka National Forest was a predecessor to the Gallatin and Custer forests. The community of Absarokee grew up near the site of the second Crow Agency. The Agency moved

RICK GRAETZ

from Mission Creek, near Livingston, to this site in 1875; in 1882 it moved to the present Crow Agency, south of Hardin.

Absaroka has survived on today's landscape, but the Crow name "Na piet say" has not. Meaning "the bear's tooth," Na piet say referred to a sharp snag that juts from the jaw of Beartooth Mountain in the eastern part of the range. Its unmistakable profile is seen by travelers on the Red Lodge-Cooke City Highway.

The name Beartooth has been given to many other features: a lake, a mountain, a butte, a creek, a falls, and a highway. Most importantly, it has been given to the mountain range—the Beartooth!

Technically, the Beartooth is a section of the Absaroka Range, extending from Livingston southeastward to the canyon of the Clarks Fork of the Yellowstone. The northeastern edge is hemmed by plains and the western border is the Yellowstone River. Although the southern border is less distinct, it is commonly defined by the Yellowstone River and its tributaries Soda Butte Creek and the Clarks Fork of the Yellowstone. Most of Yellowstone Park is considered to lie south of the Beartooth.

Much of the Beartooth is in Montana. In Wyoming, the range encompasses the lakes area north of the Red Lodge-Cooke City Highway, the plateau that spills into the canyon of the Clarks Fork of the Yellowstone River, and the lower reaches of Hellroaring Creek, Buffalo Fork, and Slough Creek.

PAUL VUCETICH

The Beartooth is not without its component ranges. The series of 12,000-foot peaks around and including Granite Peak has been known as the Granite Range. The mountains on the west side of Paradise Valley south of Livingston were once known as the Yellowstone Range. Later they were called the Snowy (or Snow) Range. Geologists now refer to that section as the North Snowy Block. Local residents call the range the Absarokas, ignoring the far southern extent of that range.

Above: *The view into Sunlight Basin (on right side) from Dead Indian Pass.*

Facing page: *Rough Lake, with Granite Peak's south face in background.*

GEOLOGY

The earth was born 4 or 5 billion years ago. As the swirling mass of magnetic brimstone cooled, a crust and the first continents coalesced. One of these, "Beartoothia," was destined to spawn the Beartooth Mountains, but only after a long and fascinating chronology of geologic processes and events, many of which are only now becoming understood.

The time when the first rocks were formed is known as the Archean period, knowledge of which is limited because much of the geological evidence from the period has been obliterated by the many forceful events of the last 3 billion years. Most Archean rocks lie buried beneath other rocks, both sedimentary and igneous.

The Beartooth Mountains, one of the best examples of exposed Archean rocks on earth, provide geologists with a unique laboratory for solving the puzzles of the earth's early events. Not only is most of the range a naked, uplifted block of Archean rocks, but these rocks are exposed vertically by the deep glaciated canyons. Furthermore, the Beartooth Highway provides excellent access to this natural laboratory. The result is a wealth of literature on the

Above: Twin Lakes and Beartooth Pass.

Facing page: Mount Republic.

geology of the Beartooth Mountains. This literature dates from the late 1800s, and is especially rich beginning in the 1930s, when the Princeton Geology Camp (now the Yellowstone Bighorn Research Association) was established at Red Lodge.

About some things there has been agreement from the beginning: the Beartooth Mountains resulted from the uplifting of an Archean (early Precambrian) block of metamorphic rocks; these rocks were eroded and glaciated and, on their southwest corner, covered with volcanic rocks during the Tertiary period.

On many other aspects of the geology of the Beartooth, knowledge has developed slowly and theories have come and gone. For example, the origin of the Archean rocks was thought for decades to be sediments laid down by the earth's early seas. Current thinking favors an origin based on the intrusion of magma, later granite, into early sediments.

After the birth of the earth, the continents were formed by thickening of the crust, accomplished in most cases by separation of light crust from the mantle via igneous processes. In other places, perhaps in the north-

JOHN REDDY

west corner of the Beartooth, the thickening was caused tectonically, by the moving of large sections of the earth's crust.

Following the formation of the continent Beartoothia, the earth was covered by seas filled with murky sediments. These sediments were deposited on the continental crust-forming rocks that were subject to erosion. For the next billion years, the Archean rocks were formed, by sedimentation or by cooling of magmatic material, then destroyed by erosion, altered by heat and pressure, folded, intruded, and buried. All this took place during the 2 billion years that preceded the first of the region's two most dramatic geologic events.

About 2.8 billion years ago, a major metamorphism took place. Archean rocks—sedimentary, igneous, and metamorphic alike—underwent a massive, region-wide transformation. Schists and related rocks were formed from the sediments; gneisses and similar rocks were formed from the igneous ones. At about the same time, 2.75 to 2.8 million years ago, into what is now the eastern two thirds of the Beartooth, a granitic magma, called the Beartooth batholith, was intruded into the Archean rocks. Then, along the northern edge of the present Beartooth, a body of igneous magma—the Stillwater Complex—was injected into the country rock. The Stillwater Complex is now fault-bounded, having been turned to a nearly vertical orientation.

This Beartooth orogeny, or mountain building, was a regional, deformational metamorphic igneous event that established much of what may be observed in the Beartooth today. The faults and fractures established at that time formed a pattern for the faulting and uplifting that made the Beartooth into mountains, over 2.5 billion years later. Many of those rocks formed during

the Beartooth orogeny can be seen from the Beartooth Highway.

Beginning during the Beartooth orogeny, several periods of intrusion at 2.6, 2.2, 2.0, 1.3, and 0.8 billion years ago left mafic dikes in fractures and faults. Mafic rocks, igneous ones low in silica and high in iron and magnesium, can be recognized by their extremely dark color.

The latest intrusion occurred in the Tertiary period, perhaps as recently as 30 million years ago.

After the Beartooth orogeny, things were peaceful—by Precambrian standards—for some time. Only infrequent

Above: Buffalo Meadows.
Left: Lone Elk Lake, the Sawtooth Spires and Mount Villard.
Top left: From Sundance Pass, looking west.

Facing page: Beartooth Plateau.

Map by Ed Madej

The Beartooth Range Geology

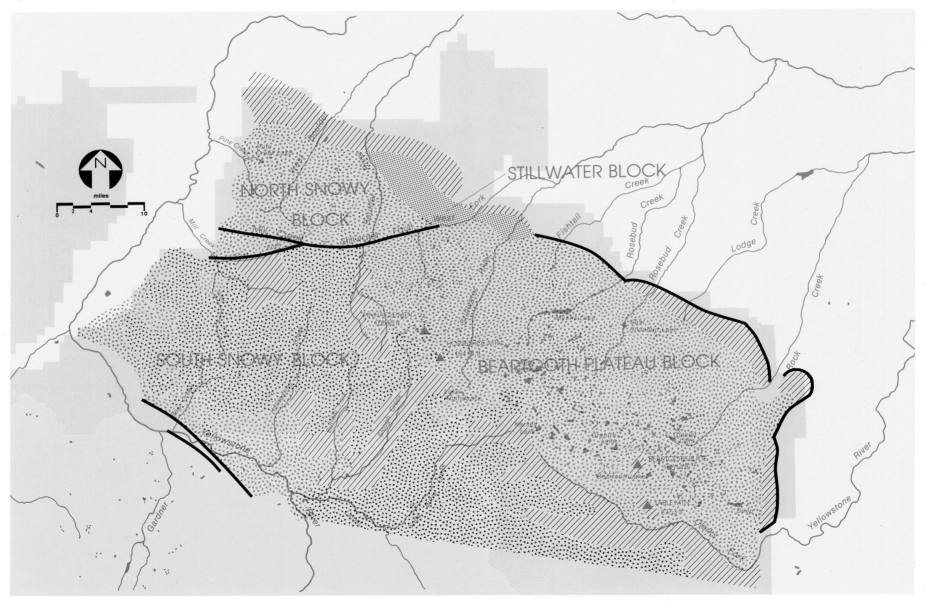

Stillwater Complex ⋰   **Tertiary Volcanic Rocks** ⋰   **Paleozoic Sedimentary Rocks** ⫽   **Precambrian Rocks** ⋇   **Major Fault Lines** ▬

metamorphic events and occasional periods of folding, faulting, and igneous intrusion occurred. Incessantly, however, forces of erosion nibbled at the rocks, creating a surface onto which sediments would later be laid.

In mid-Cambrian time, about 530 million years ago, most of North America was a lowland. The eroded Precambrian surfaces were inundated by warm seas, then covered with the first of a series of Paleozoic sedimentary rocks, the Flathead sandstone. On top of this came other Cambrian strata: Wolsey, Meagher, Park, Maurice, Grove Creek, and Snowy Range.

Following the Cambrian rocks came the Ordovician Bighorn limestone, then the Devonian sequence: the Beartooth Butte, the Jefferson, and the Threeforks. And so on, through millions of years, thousands of feet, and untold lost stories of the drama of the evolution of the planet, its rocks, and its life forms. Abundant evidence of the deposition of the sedimentary strata, largely absent from the Beartooth massif itself, may be seen in many places on the periphery of the range.

About 65 million years ago, during late Cretaceous time, the second major event occurred in the development of the Beartooth Range—the

Laramide Orogeny. Up and down the North American continent, great plates in the earth's crust were forced together. The resulting compressional forces were irresistible—the earth's crust had nowhere to go but up.

The uplift occurred in two stages, interrupted by a quiescent mid-Tertiary period. The first stage lasted from early Paleocene time (about 61 million years ago) to early Eocene time (about 52 million years ago). The second stage began in late Miocene or early Pliocene time (15 to 5 million years ago) and continues today.

Three distinct blocks had been thrust upwards

Sundance Glacier.

GEORGE WUERTHNER

Looking toward Mount Rearguard.

RICK GRAETZ

Above: Whitetail Peak and Ship Lake.

Facing page, top left: From above Lulu Pass, looking north toward Mount Wolf to the left, Mount Zimmer in the middle.
Top right: Cross-country skiing above Rough Lake—Granite Peak in background.
Bottom: Below the summit of Whitetail Peak, looking south.

from the Bighorn basin on the east. The largest block, the Beartooth Block, had risen the highest—nearly 20,000 feet. On the west side of the range the North and South Snowy blocks had risen almost as far.

As the mountains were being uplifted, there were also moved horizontally and rotationally. The main Beartooth Block was tilted southwestward and thrust ten to twelve miles northeastward. The Snowy blocks in the west were tilted northeastward and thrust to the southwest.

On the margins of the range, the sediments were uplifted, locally overturned, and thrust over the adjacent basins on high angle reverse faults. On the bulk of the uplift, the sedimentary rocks are only locally preserved as erosional remnants.

As the Laramide Orogeny ebbed, another violent chapter dawned. Volcanoes began to erupt in the Yellowstone-Absaroka belt that extends from near the southwest corner of Yellowstone National Park to the Gallatin Valley and includes the western and central part of the Beartooth Range. Billions of tons of molten rock were spewed into the air, oozed onto the surface, and intruded into the many cracks and fissures left by the Laramide mountain-building. Much of the South Snowy Block was covered with volcanic rocks giving it the appearance of the Gallatin Range to the west and the Absaroka Range to the south.

Late in the Tertiary period, through the Miocene and Pliocene epochs, the mountains continued to uplift, rapidly enough to outpace erosion. The result was a net increase in the elevation of the landscape. But erosion was effective. Nearly all the sediments

were stripped from the largest of the uplifts, the Beartooth Block. An exception occurs at Beartooth Butte where a monadnock (an outlier of sediments), representing some 200 million years' accumulation, escaped. In a few other places on the Precambrian metamorphic rocks, remnants of the Flathead sandstone, the first layer deposited in Cambrian times, may be found.

As the curtain fell on the Pliocene epoch of the Tertiary, the Quaternary period began. For 1 or 2 million years, the temperature of the earth fell and the highlands and the northern lowlands became arctic and were covered with ice. Huge sheets of ice ebbed and flowed as the climate fluctuated. Glaciers sculpted the mountains, carving nests, protected from the heat of the southern sun.

There were at least three major periods of glaciation in the northern Rockies. The first was called the "Buffalo," for the Buffalo Fork of the Snake River where its leavings were first described. The second and third, the Bull Lake and the Pinedale, peaked about 150,000 and 25,000 years ago, respectively. Named for locations in Wyoming's Wind River Range where they were described in the early part of this century, these glacial periods put the finishing touches on the Beartooth Range, on northern Yellowstone Park, and on the upper Yellowstone Valley.

Because of its high elevation, the Beartooth was the source of a giant sheet of ice that flowed south across the plateau, then west through the valleys of Soda Butte Creek and the Lamar River, then north into the upper Yellowstone Valley. So powerful was this glacier, it flowed upstream into the drainages of Sunlight Basin and left moraines of granite in valleys with volcanic rocks at their heads.

Much of the Beartooth Plateau was covered with ice. On the south flank of the plateau, the topography is rolling. The ice scraped the rock clean, leaving little debris. The highest peaks escaped the ice, as did a few refuges on the south side of the range. On the north slopes, the ice quickly gouged U-shaped canyons into the rock and created the alternating plateau-canyon landscape.

Between 4,000 and 7,000 years ago, there occurred a warming trend in the prevailing glacial climate. Called the Altithermal Period, this era saw the demise of the great glaciers. Since that time, two minor glacial advances, known collectively as the "Little Ice Age," have occurred. The most recent lasted until about 1920. Remnants of this period, such as Grasshopper Glacier near Cooke City, can be seen today, although they are fast disappearing

The geologic history of the Beartooth is long and dramatic and is still being written. The landscape is continually being altered by active processes. Tiny glaciers are grinding into the bedrock. Landslides sweep from the steep slopes of glacial canyon walls. Water continues to dissolve and erode the durable crystalline rocks. Wind gnaws at unprotected slopes. The annual (and sometimes daily) cycle of freezing and thawing incessantly cleaves even the strongest rocks. And amid this flux of physical forces, tiny, subterranean fingers of alpine plants search relentlessly for invisible cracks.

BEARTOOTH BUTTE

A glance at scenic Beartooth Butte raises a question to the astute observer: What is a sedimentary mountain doing on this glaciated plateau of crystalline rocks?

The answer, not an entirely satisfactory one, is that the butte is a remnant of the sedimentary strata that covered the entire plateau, even before it was a plateau, when it was part of the extensive bed of an inland sea that covered much of North America. But why, after the uplift of the Beartooth block, was this remnant spared from erosion by running water, scouring by ice, and sliding induced by gravity that removed the surrounding sediments?

Beartooth Butte isn't the only such remnant. Clay Butte to the west and Table Mountain to the south are similar. They, however, are no less remarkable in their survival of the ice age. Beartooth Butte is the most interesting of these sedimentary survivors, however. Its strata reveal a 1,200-foot calendar of Paleozoic rocks. From bottom to top they are Cambrian quartzite, shale, limestone and flat-pebble conglomerate, Ordovician dolomite, and Devonian limestone. Most of these rocks are marine, the result of the settling of fine particles through the seas that covered the area. In the central portion of the eastern scarp face, above the older Ordovician dolomite and below the younger chocolate-colored Devonian limestone, there is a remarkable outcrop of a red, gray, and yellow shaly limestone, lower Devonian in age.

This lens, the cross-section of a stream channel or estuary, penetrates the butte and emerges on the other side. In it are the fossils of both fish and plants that lived 400 million years ago.

In 1930, a party from the Princeton Research Project, headquartered in Red Lodge, made a reconnaissance trip to Beartooth Butte. Among those on the trip was Erling Dorf, a member of the Princeton University faculty. Returning in 1931, the geologists climbed the butte and descended its east face. In the talus below the shaly limestone, they discovered several fish plates. Later in the summer, Dorf and a few of his students returned to the butte and collected fossils from the outcrop itself.

Among the vertebrate fossils were 29 species, mostly Ostracoderms, or bony-plated fishes. Also found were fossils of the most primitive terrestrial plants, the Psiliphytales. At the time, they were the oldest known plants ever found in North America.

Writing in 1934, Dorf summarized the unusual nature of the fossil deposits. First, the rocks seemed to be sediments from a freshwater environment, unusual in the dominantly marine formations of the middle Rocky Mountains Paleozoic strata. Second, the deposit yielded an uncommonly rich fish fauna. Third, the small but well-preserved flora was the first evidence of land plants in the Paleozoic rocks of the Middle Rocky Mountains. Lastly, lower Devonian sediments had not previously been found in this region.

Erling Dorf, then in his thirties, went on to distinguish himself as a geologist and climatologist, serving forty-eight years as a Princeton professor. The Princeton Geology Camp he founded, along with Walter Bucher and W.T. Thom, became the Yellowstone Bighorn Research Association, which is still active today. One of Dorf's interests over the years was the petrified forests of the Absaroka range of the Yellowstone region. He maintained his interest in the Beartooth, spending his last summers in Red Lodge at the YBRA. He died in 1984 at age seventy-eight.

GLACIATION

When it's winter in the Beartooth, half of the earth's land and a third of its ocean surfaces are covered with ice and snow. A tenth of the earth's land surface is covered with glacial ice, which stores three fourths of all fresh surface water.

Although glaciers command a major presence on today's earth, the glacial era in the Beartooth is in recession. However, the Beartooth landscape is vivid with its history of glacial activity. There is ample evidence of intervals of glaciation as far back as Precambrian time, millions, even billions of years ago. The latest glaciation, the "Little Ice Age," lasted until about 1920.

Glaciers are mostly ice crystals, but also contain air, water, and rock debris. Because the hexagonal ice crystals are weak, they slip easily on planes parallel to the base of a glacier. The component of the force of gravity parallel to that surface leads to deformation and flow.

Both primary glacial forms, valley (alpine) and continental (shield), have played prominent roles in the sculpting of the Beartooth. On the south side of the Beartooth Plateau, a shield-type glacier carved the undulating shape seen today. On the north side of the range, valley glaciers incised the bedrock into spectacular U-shaped canyons with nearly vertical walls in many places.

Glaciers erode rocks in two ways: abrasion and plucking (also known as quarrying or joint-block removal). Abrasion occurs when bedrock is scored by the grit between the surfaces of the ice and the rock. The evidence that remains includes grooves and scratches (striations). The process of plucking or quarrying is less well understood, but the craggy knobs that result are plentiful in the Beartooth.

On the Beartooth Plateau evidence of both processes abounds. "Roches moutonees" (rock sheep)—streamlined hills with gentle, abraded up-ice slopes and steep, plucked down-ice faces—are characteristic of glaciation the world over, and common on the Beartooth Plateau.

Another worldwide glacial characteristic is the cirque, a basin presently or formerly occupied by the head of a valley glacier. Armchair shaped, cirques have steep headwalls, gently sloping floors, and often contain glacial lakes. Cirques are enlarged by freeze-thaw action in the headwall and deepened by the rotational abrasion of the glacial ice.

In the north temperate latitudes, as in Montana and Wyoming, cirques usually face between north and east. Where cirques back up to each other, either horns or arêtes are formed. Horns, like Switzerland's Matterhorn, are isolated peaks with three or four distinct faces. Some horns are connected with ridges (arêtes).

Moraines, the debris left by glacial sculpting, are low ridges of till (unsorted, unstratified sediment) that can take one of several forms. They may be lateral—alongside a glacier; they may be medial—between glaciers; and they may be terminal—at the end of the advance of a glacier. All types can be seen in the Beartooth, particularly on the north side of the range.

Glaciers tend to perpetuate themselves, even in eras of warm climate. In northeast-facing cirques, they are protected from the energy of the sun. Snowfall blown into these cirques in the winter tends to be incorporated into the ice of the glaciers instead of being melted by the summer sun. So, the glaciers create the cirques and the cirques in turn provide a favorable habitat for the glaciers.

PERIGLACIATION

The massive uplift and the subsequent glacial sculpting of the Beartooth Mountains are impressive in their grandeur. The geological story of the Beartooth still is being written, however. All across the face of the plateau one marvels at the ever-forming evidence of the day-to-day work done by wind, water, and ice.

The term "periglacial" was introduced early in

Above: Looking down Rough Draw toward ridge to Livingston Peak and Mission Creek.
Top: Glacial erratic at Beartooth Pass.
Right: Sunset lights Clay Butte.

Facing page: Granite Peak.

this century to designate the climate and the climatically-controlled features adjacent to the Pleistocene ice sheets. Gradually the term was expanded to include nonglacial processes and features of cold climates. The most prevalent of these processes is frost action, including cracking, wedging, heaving, and sorting.

The forces generated by the action of frost are exerted in all directions, but because of the physical constraints of the ground, they are manifested either upwardly (heaving) or horizontally (thrusting). As these forces are exerted, particles of all sizes are displaced. Huge boulders may be uplifted from below the surface or small soil particles may creep as a part of a larger mass.

Several complex and poorly understood frost-related processes contribute to the generation of patterns on the ground. The many striking manifestations of frost forces, among them differential frost heaving, thawing, mass-wasting, and weathering, are patterns variously categorized as nets, circles, polygons, steps, and stripes.

Circles, nets, and stripes normally occur on nearly horizontal ground. Stripes and steps are found on slopes. Any of these patterns may be either sorted or unsorted. In the case of sorting,

the pattern has a border of stones. Patterned ground, common on the Beartooth Plateau, may even be seen on the bottoms of shallow lakes.

Other common frost-related features are found in the Beartooth. Creep is the ratchet-like movement of a mass of particles caused by the heaving of frozen ground perpendicular to the slope surface, followed by the vertical settling after the seasonal thaw. Solifluction is the slow, downslope flow of soil saturated with water. When frost is involved, the process is called gelifluction.

Yet another periglacial feature common to the Beartooth is one with an oxymoronic name: rock glacier. Is it a glacier or is it a rock? Rock glaciers, lobe-like bodies of rock and perhaps ice resembling true ice glaciers, originate in high mountain catchment basins much like glacial cirques. The headwall of the basin is usually steep, providing a good source of loose rock. The slope of the basin floor is gentle.

The longitudinal cross-section of a typical rock glacier shows glacial ice at the base, in contact with the bedrock. Covering the ice is a layer of ice-cemented rubble. Mantling this layer is loose rock. The upper surface is lobed and the frontal scarp is steep—at the angle of repose.

Sometime in the past, and perhaps continuing into the present, the rock glacier has moved downslope, due to the flow and deformation of the ice in the core. Evidence of past movement is the undulating upper surface. Present movement is demonstrated by the occasional overturning of rocks on the surface. Rocks with lichens on the underside are evidence of such movement.

Among those who appreciate a good rock glacier are the pikas. The surface rocks provide ideal dens and cover and nearby meadows are their grocery stores.

PERMAFROST

Permafrost, or permanently frozen ground, underlies more than one fifth of the world's land area. Usually associated with arctic environments, permafrost frequently occurs in the high mountains at lower latitudes. Over a hundred years ago, miners and engineers in mineral-rich alpine areas such as the Beartooth learned that mine shafts penetrated permafrost.

Permafrost forms where the mean annual air temperature is below freezing. The depth of winter frost penetration then exceeds the depth of summer thaw. The permafrost thickens until a balance is reached between the heat transferred from the earth and the heat lost to the atmosphere.

Permafrost is affected by many factors, the most important being mean annual temperature and wind speed, both of which affect the transfer of heat from the earth to the atmosphere and vice versa. The nature of the surface also is important, because heat transfer is affected by soil moisture, soil color, snow, and vegetation. The interrelation of these variables is complex and some can act as both causes and effects.

Because of its direct relationship to mean annual temperature, permafrost commonly occurs above the treeline in boggy areas in arctic and alpine situations. One notable and interesting exception might be found on the southern flank of the Beartooth Plateau.

Near Sawtooth Mountain is a bed of peat, with underlying permafrost. For decades, cowboys, sheepherders, prospectors, and hunters have used the frozen beds to refrigerate camp supplies. The peat bed measures about 20,000 feet by 1,500 feet, an area of more than 50 acres, and is estimated to be 10 to 15 feet thick. In several places, ice and frozen peat occur a foot and a half below the surface. In these areas, because the temperature is so cold year round, no vegetation grows on the exposed peat surface.

During the past ice age, deep valleys adjacent to the bed were filled with ice, but the peat deposit escaped glaciation. Although this site has a mean annual air temperature above freezing, the peat has insulated the frozen ground, thus preventing enough heat transfer to melt the ice.

In places, uneven ground has permitted thawing of the permafrost. Water in the resulting depressions has kept the underlying peat wet and permitted downward thawing to continue during the summer months. The irregular topography that results is called "thermokarst"; the depressions are known as thaw depressions, thaw ponds, or cave-in lakes. Several can be seen at the Sawtooth peat bed.

Great gaps exist in our knowledge of the detailed geographic distribution of permafrost and of the precise relationships among the various climatic parameters, climatic history, controlling terrestrial factors, and the subsurface thermal gradient. In the case of the Sawtooth permafrost, exceptional for its sub-treeline location, the most important factor is the insulation provided by the peat.

STILLWATER COMPLEX

One of the most strategic metals in today's technological society is chromium, necessary for the manufacture of stainless steel. Virtually all of the chromium consumed in this country has been imported, due to the low cost of those imports. During the two world wars, however, America was forced to turn inward for chrome. Eighty percent of the chrome reserves in the United States are found in the Beartooth Mountains, in the

Stillwater Complex, south of Columbus and Absarokee.

The Stillwater Complex is a band of igneous rocks that were intruded into the basement rocks during the Precambrian age, 2.7 billion years ago. About a mile in thickness, the complex extends continuously along the northern flank of the Beartooth Range for thirty miles, bounded by faults at each end. Its western extent can be seen in the canyon of the Main Boulder River; toward the east, it cuts across the East Boulder River, the West Fork of the Stillwater River, the Stillwater River, and stops short of Fishtail Creek.

The Stillwater Complex is remarkable because it is layered, much like sedimentary rocks. The stratification, a series of alternating, metal-rich bands of silicate minerals, is due to the differential settling of molten minerals as they slowly cooled. The resulting rainbow of minerals includes—in addition to chrome—platinum, palladium, rhodium, copper, nickel, and iron. Chrome-rich bands are found in layers near the base of the deposit. Platinum-group metals are found in several layers; the one with the highest concentration is barely a meter thick. Lust for these minerals has led to serious exploration and some development for more than a hundred years.

In 1851, an agreement with several Indian tribes was signed at Fort Laramie. This so-called treaty was considered a breakthrough in the taming of the west, even though it was never legally adopted by the President and the Crow were not a party to it. One of its effects was to enhance the sense of ownership the Crow had in the Yellowstone basin. From the "bend of the river" (present-day Livingston) to the Powder River, the Yellowstone was Crow country.

The settling of Montana by whites occurred during the Civil War. Prospectors from the gold fields of Idaho, learning of gold discoveries, swarmed into Bannack, then Alder Gulch. But there wasn't room for everyone; the ambitious and the idle, guided by rumors, fanned into the countryside, notably the mountains.

The most intriguing area was the upper Yellowstone. It was "owned" by the Crow and was off limits to whites. Suspecting the presence of minerals in this forbidden land, several surreptitious parties explored the canyons and gulches. One of the finds was the Stillwater Complex.

In 1875 Crow Agency was moved from Mission Creek near present-day Livingston to the Stillwater Valley south of Absarokee, giving prospectors more security to explore the north face of the Beartooth. A treaty in 1880, negotiated as a result of pressure from business interests in Bozeman and Cooke City, was promulgated in 1882; it released the upper Yellowstone to the whites and legitimized the mining activity at Emigrant Gulch, Bear Gulch, and Cooke City. And also, thought some, in the Stillwater Complex.

In 1883, Jack Nye and two brothers named Hedges, having been prospecting in the Stillwater, arrived in Bozeman with "proof" of a lead of copper-bearing ore that they said was fifteen miles long. By 1884, Nye had interested the Minnesota Mining Company in the prospect. In 1887, the town of Nye was founded and by 1889 a smelter was erected, 5,000 feet of tunneling had been completed, and $200,000 had been spent. Then the curtain fell, even more quickly than it had been raised. In 1888, the Secretary of the Interior issued an order closing the camp—Nye was within the boundaries of the Crow Reservation. At the nascent age of one year, Nye City was a ghost town, not for the usual reason of mineral depletion, but from a rare "administrative" cause of death.

Though the Crows relinquished the remainder of the Beartooth in 1891, the Stillwater Complex was quiet until 1905. T.C. "Chalk" Benbow, fresh from the 1904 St. Louis exposition where he had failed in his quest for a prize with his passenger balloon (see page 48), looked for his fortune in the mountains. He found the largest chrome deposit in the western hemisphere, but the grade was so low he couldn't interest anyone in the development.

With the outbreak of the first world war, the federal government became interested in developing a domestic supply of chromium. In 1917, exploration took place near the Benbow mine, but no ore was shipped and interest waned.

In 1933, seven claims in the Benbow group were patented. In 1939, with the outbreak of the second world war, the U.S. Bureau of Mines and the U.S. Geological Survey began an intense survey of the Stillwater Complex. Results were favorable—in 1941, the government hired the Anaconda Company to mine chrome. A mill and a mining camp were constructed at the Mouat Mine, near Nye, the Benbow property was opened, and the Gish Mine near the Main Boulder River was expanded.

Several hundred thousand tons of ore were mined for the war effort. In 1943, however, shipping lanes were freed from the predation of Nazi U-boats, chrome from South Africa once again became available, and the Stillwater project was abruptly closed. Again Nye died, this time from international politics.

Between 1953 and 1961, the American Chrome Company produced about 900,000 tons of chromite concentrate at the Mouat Mine, again under a federal contract. In the 1970s the Nixon administration sold the mine at a loss to a foreign corporation, which removed it from the site.

Above: *The main Boulder River.*
Right top: *In the Absaroka Range near Elephant Head.*
Right: *View southeast to Mineral Mountain from Emigrant Peak.*

Facing page: *Mount Wood (center).*

In 1967, a mining geologist for the Johns-Manville Company made a startling discovery–the Stillwater Complex was also rich in platinum and palladium. Again, the boom was on.

Platinum is used as a catalyst in pollution devices, especially automotive catalytic converters required by the Clean Air Act of 1990, and in jewelry; 1989 worldwide demand was 3.4 million troy ounces. Palladium is used in space age electronics microcircuitry, as a catalyst in the chemical industry, and in dental alloys; 1989 worldwide demand was 3.3 million troy ounces. U.S. demand covers about half the total.

After 1967, exploration continued, holes were drilled, ore was tested in pilot plants, and mining companies negotiated with state and federal agencies and each other. The Stillwater Mining Company, a partnership of Manville Mining Company and Chevron U.S.A., received approval to mine in 1985. In 1986, production began. At 1,000 tons per day, the mine is the only economically viable platinum/palladium mine in the western hemisphere and accounts for 5 percent of world production.

The ore is upgraded on site by crushing, grinding, floating, and drying to obtain a concentrate that is shipped by truck to a smelter in Columbus

for processing to the matte stage. The smelted matte is shipped to Belgium for refining.

About 62 percent of tailings created by milling is returned underground as backfill. The remaining 38 percent goes to a lined impoundment adjacent to the mine and mill facility. In 1992 the company received approval to expand production to 2,000 tons per day.

In the meantime, the Stillwater Mining Company began to explore the East Boulder River area of the Stillwater Complex. After the issuance of an environmental impact statement, the company received permission to mine in 1993.

After over a century, Jack Nye finally has his proof.

DEEP LAKE

Most Beartooth lakes are glacial in origin. A few, like East Rosebud Lake, are formed by dams made by alluvial fans deposited by side streams. Even fewer were created by dams resulting from landslides. Deep Lake is an example of this phenomenon. And what a landslide it must have been!

Littlerock Creek flows from the Beartooth Plateau and joins the Clarks Fork of the Yellowstone River at the site of the Bannock Indian battle. Midway in its journey, the canyon steepens, the result of a glacial incision. An over-steepened wall was left on an arced surface in the smooth Precambrian rocks on the north face of the canyon. In a spectacular release of energy and mass, the slope gave way and rushed into the canyon, blocking the stream with an 800-foot-high dam, forming Deep Lake a mile and a half long, and depositing debris at least a mile from the release zone. Littlerock Creek is now denied surface passage by the bulkhead, and issues from the east face of the dam as a series of springs.

One of the largest and least accessible lakes in the Beartooth Mountains, Deep Lake is about a mile downstream from the site of the former Camp Sawtooth.

People in the Past

The history of man's occupation and use of the Absaroka and Beartooth mountains began long before conscious record-keeping became common practice. Therefore, little evidence of people can be found that predates 1800.

There probably were primitive people in the mountains when conditions were favorable. After the retreat of the great ice sheets—10,000 to 12,000 years ago—hunters inhabited the plains. Although the mountains still harbored glaciers, high ridges, such as in Buffalo Fork and Hellroaring, were ice-free at this time. Arrowheads and other tools found there attest to the presence of primitive people.

From about 5,000 B.C. to 2,000 B.C., during a great drought known as the Altithermal Period, survival was even more difficult than usual for the early residents of North America. The mountains, however, may have been spared the drastic drying that seared the plains.

About 3,000 B.C., a landslide dammed the Yellowstone River at Yankee Jim Canyon, creating a lake that extended upstream to where Gardiner perches today. The lake shore provided forage and shelter for the hardy people who made it their home. Campfire rings found in the vicinity of Corwin Springs show that people lived there from 2,600 B.C. to 500 B.C.

Over the last few centuries, the plains and mountains have been inhabited by Native Americans. Because they left no written records, little is known about their ways of life. We can surmise, however, that they had dynamic, evolving cultures with various tribes competing for space and food. By the 1800s, this competition intensified due to the westward pressure exerted by the growing white society. The displacement of tribes in the eastern United States produced a ripple effect felt far onto the western plains.

In the 1700s, the Hidatsa nation occupied a territory centered in present-day North Dakota. An intertribal dispute split the Hidatsa into two new tribes—the Crow and the Minataree. During this period, the Hidatsa acquired horses, giving them the mobility and versatility that enabled them to successfully emigrate to the west. They eventually occupied the "Valley of the Yellow Rocks."

The Crows found the Yellowstone Valley to be an ideal home. It offered an optimal combination of plains and mountains to meet the year-round needs of the tribe. It produced abundant grass and water. Most importantly, it was home to bountiful wildlife: bison on the prairie; beaver in the streams; elk, deer, and antelope in the foothills; and bear and sheep in the Absaroka, Beartooth, Pryor, and Bighorn mountains.

The Yellowstone Valley provided the Crows all they desired—except exclusive title. The region's riches were coveted by many neighbors. The Blackfeet, living to the west and known as a hostile and ever-warring tribe, gave the Crows the most trouble.

The Bannock culture of the Snake River plain to the southwest of the Beartooth subsisted on bison. But around 1840 the bison disappeared and the Bannock began annual hunting trips to the plains. These migrations took the Bannocks through the geyser basin, across Cooke Pass, and down the Clarks Fork, bringing them into direct confrontation with the Crows and other plains groups.

The Sheepeaters were the only natives who lived year-round in the mountains and on the Yellowstone Plateau. Unmounted and docile, they didn't compete well with the other tribes. Many whites thought of the Sheepeaters as weak, harmless, and feebleminded. It is more likely that their way of life was not well understood due to their timidity. Osborn Russell, the articulate trapper, held them in high regard.

Many other tribes possessed at least a passing acquaintance with the mountains of the Beartooth. Among them were the Shoshone, the Sioux, the Cheyenne, the Arapaho, the Nez Perce, the Gros Ventre, and the Flathead. By and large, however, the Yellowstone country was home to the Crow, at least until internal strife divided the tribal family. Sometime around 1850, one faction, the River Crow, moved north to the Missouri; the Mountain Crow stayed in the Yellowstone Valley.

The first white people seen by the natives were the explorers, who seemed harmless. Understanding the odds of surviving fights against overwhelming numbers, the early explorers tended to rely more on stealth, diplomacy and trade than on coercion.

The first white explorers to approach the Beartooth were probably Chevalier de la Verendrye and his brother, two French Canadians in pursuit of their father's dream of reaching the Pacific from Montreal. Their report, weak on geographical detail, has been interpreted as placing them as far upstream as the Gates of the Mountains on the Missouri in 1837. More likely, they got no farther west than the Bighorn Mountains.

Meanwhile, wars and politics in Europe were setting the stage for a new era in the northern Rockies. In 1762, at the end of the French and American War, France ceded the midwestern part of the North American continent to Spain in one of a long series of maneuvers aimed at containing the influence of the British in North America. In 1800, Spain returned the property to France, which sold it to the United States in 1803. The $15 million Louisiana Purchase doubled the size of the young nation and launched the historic expedition of Lewis and Clark.

The glories of the Beartooth range were first viewed by William Clark and his party on July 15, 1806, crossing Bozeman Pass from the west. They camped that night on the Yellowstone River just downstream from present-day Livingston. Clark was intrigued by the river and its upstream canyon, but he was obliged to hurry to his rendezvous with Meriwether Lewis at the confluence of the Missouri and the Yellowstone. It was left to expedition member John Colter to later explore the headwaters of the Yellowstone.

Colter left Lewis and Clark at the Mandan villages on the Missouri, joined trappers Joseph Dickson and Forest Handcock, and headed west. The following spring, Colter again descended the Missouri and, at the mouth of the Platte, encountered Manuel Lisa, an enterprising merchant who lusted for the furs of the Rocky Mountains. Lisa persuaded Colter to join him.

In the fall of 1807, Lisa established Fort Raymond at the mouth of the Bighorn River. After the post was secure, Colter was sent out to drum up business. Carrying a seventy-pound pack, he spent the winter traveling the canyons, valley, and headwaters of the Green, Snake, and Yellowstone rivers.

The exact route of Colter's journey is not known. A map published in 1814 by William Clark shows it clearly, but the map's inaccurate topographic detail makes it impossible to ascertain where Colter actually went. That map and Colter's stories about the geysers and hot springs of the upper Yellowstone are the only testimonies to his trip.

Conventional—if unsupported—wisdom holds that John Colter explored the area that is now Yellowstone National Park and, on his return to the mouth of the Bighorn, crossed the pass at the heads of the Soda Butte Creek and the Clarks Fork River near today's Cooke City. That would have made him the first white man to visit the Beartooth Mountains.

The following years, until 1840, comprised the era of the fur trapper in the northern Rockies. Like the natives, trappers left little evidence of their presence. Few were literate. Most rationalized the strenuous trapper's life in measures of freedom and unaccountability.

One exception to the trapper stereotype was Osborn Russell, who was both literate and articulate. Russell traveled and trapped in the Northern Rockies during the 1830s with the likes of Jim Bridger. His journal, with maps and editing by Aubrey Haines, former historian at Yellowstone National Park, places him in and around the Beartooth and Absaroka mountains. Later in life, Russell became a successful politician in Oregon and California.

Johnston Gardiner lived and trapped in the upper Yellowstone as early as the 1820s. His favorite spot, where he lived in bliss for decades, was where a river and town bear his name (with different spellings).

Prior to 1825, the fur companies controlled the trapping business in monopolistic fashion. After the War of 1812, however, the trade in furs waned in response to the declining popularity of beaver hats. When trading posts became unprofitable, the Rocky Mountain Fur Company created a clever alternative that served both the economic and social interest of the trappers—the annual rendezvous, at which they gathered to trade, drink, make love, renew acquaintances, fight, and lie. The first was held on the Green River in 1825. Later rendezvous were held at various places around the northern Rockies. The last occurred in 1840, when the fur trade was virtually dead and almost no young trappers were being recruited into the business. For the next two decades, the mountains and plains once again belonged exclusively to the natives. Other forces were taking shape, however; in the east, men of vision were talking about a transcontinental railroad.

After two decades of this debate, Jefferson Davis, the Secretary of War under President Franklin Pierce, sent out several survey parties in the 1850s. Governor Stevens of Washington Territory conducted the northern survey and reported favorably on a route that would link the industrial cities of the northeast with the Pacific.

Pressure for expansion in the United States led the government to increase its role in the Rocky Mountain region. Over fifty years after William

Clark brushed the north face of the Beartooth and John Colter may have passed the Plateau on the south, the Raynolds-Maynadier expedition set out to penetrate the wonders of the geyser basin reported by Colter. The guide for this 1859-60 expedition was Jim Bridger, then in his mid-fifties.

Curiously, the Raynolds effort failed to reach the Yellowstone Plateau, despite the knowledge and experience of the veteran Bridger and despite virtually circumnavigating it. Despite this failure, the expedition generated enough publicity to pique the curiosity of many, including prospectors who had heard rumors about more than steam.

During the 1860s, several parties of mineral-seeking prospectors entered the upper Yellowstone. Few records of their visits exist, partly due to the secretive nature of these men. The development of mining in Montana came from the west and the south, not from the east. After the California gold fields had become overcrowded in the 1850s, surplus miners moved on and found gold in Nevada, Utah, and Idaho. By 1860, when these areas had been overrun as well, the next convenient place to look for gold was Montana, and the logical entrance, for ease of access and minimum potential for conflict with natives, was from the south.

Though gold was first found in the Montana in 1852, it wasn't until 1863 that the bonanza at Alder Gulch was found and the rush was on. True to form, the place was soon overrun and idle miners naturally began to speculate about new prospects. The place most often mentioned was the upper Yellowstone.

At the time, the Absaroka and Beartooth mountains and the Yellowstone Valley were understood to belong to the Crows. The Treaty of 1851, unsigned by the Crows and never promul-

Left: Wagon ruts of the Bozeman Trail are still visible near Absarokee.
Below: Packstring near Rainbow Lakes.

Facing page, top: Young hikers pause above the Rainbow Lakes.
Bottom: Below Mount Wilse, looking east.

gated by the President, nevertheless had the effect of enhancing the sense of ownership the Crow felt for the region and the intolerance for intrusion by whites.

There existed, however, a route that minimized the chance of encountering hostile natives. From the community of Bozeman in the Gallatin Valley, a trail passed Chimney Rock and descended Trail Creek to Paradise Valley. From there, only Yankee Jim Canyon was a barrier to the thermal region of Yellowstone.

Prospectors soon learned that much of the up-

per Yellowstone was underlain by volcanic rock with little mineral potential. But to the north, along the contacts between these volcanic rocks and the crystalline rock of the Beartooth uplift, was plenty of promise.

In 1863, several parties ventured east from Bozeman in search of the elusive yellow metal. One was led by James Stuart of Deer Lodge, another by Walter DeLacy, and still another by George Austin. Paying placers were found in Bear Gulch, near Gardiner, and Emigrant Gulch near Chico.

Thomas Curry first uncovered the placer gold at Emigrant Gulch, where it had washed from the heights of the Beartooth. But he needed help in developing his find. In the meantime, another visionary, John Bozeman, dreamed of a shorter route from the east to the upper Yellowstone and on to the Gallatin, Madison, and Jefferson valleys.

The year 1864 saw a major influx of people to Montana. In response to the news of the discovery of gold at Alder Gulch the previous year, they came in droves, mostly in trains of wagons led by John Bozeman and Jim Bridger. Most of them continued on to the Gallatin Valley and the gold fields. Thomas Curry met Bridger's train at the mouth of the Shields River and persuaded a group of hardy men including David Shorthill and David Weaver to accompany him to the Upper Yellowstone. There, Shorthill and Weaver uncovered a paying proposition in Emigrant Gulch. The same year, John Allen and three others found gold in the Canyon of the Boulder River and at Baboon Mountain.

The discovery of gold at Alder Gulch and the sudden population of the region led to the establishment of Montana Territory in 1864. The first territorial legislature met and established nine counties; the Absaroka-Beartooth country was included in Gallatin County. Montana's first legislative assembly took several actions aimed at enhancing the economic development of the fledgling county. Sole right to mine coal on the upper Yellowstone was granted to the Red Streak Mountain Coal Company. N.P. Langford and his associates were given a charter for a stage and telegraph line from Virginia City to Emigrant Gulch.

Some who came to Montana in 1864 failed to find the milk and honey. They returned to civilization, many by floating the Yellowstone to the Missouri and on to St. Louis. Natives along the way delighted in using the boats and their occupants for target practice.

Yellowstone City, at the mouth of Emigrant Gulch, reached its zenith in 1865. It was a short-lived community. Tough winters with poor provisions and the constant fear of Indian attack were too much for the pioneers. By 1866, the place was virtually deserted. Later dredge mining obliterated all traces of the "city."

The Sioux were unhappy with the traffic of whites into the Yellowstone Valley via the Bozeman and Bridger trails. Their unrest led the army to establish a series of posts for white protection: Ft. Reno and Ft. Phil Kearney in Wyoming and Ft. C.F. Smith in Montana where the Bozeman Trail crosses the Bighorn River. These installations only served to anger the Sioux; Red Cloud led a rampage that lasted a decade. By 1868, the army pulled out, unable to support the remote outposts. A treaty gave the Sioux sole possession of most of the Yellowstone, ensuring continued hostilities between them and the Crow. Once again, the Yellowstone Valley was the domain of the natives. Not until General Miles subdued them in the winter of 1876-77 was the Yellowstone safe for white settlement.

John Bozeman's career was terminated prematurely in 1867 when, at the age of 30, he was killed by Blackfeet in an ambush near Mission Creek, just east of present-day Livingston. Surviving the attack was Tom Coover, who stumbled wounded into the camp of McKenzie, Reshaw, and Freeman. Leigh Freeman was a journalist who filed some of the first accounts of the thermal basin of Yellowstone.

Despite the war in the Yellowstone Valley, the upper Yellowstone was explored and prospected by adventurers from Bozeman, Helena, and Alder Gulch. Minerals were found at the Clarks Fork (later the New World Mining District and Cooke City) and Bear Gulch. Reports of the thermal wonders of Yellowstone began to return with the explorers. Interest in the geysers grew until a series of expeditions was launched: the Folsom-Cook trip of 1869, the Washburn-Doane effort of 1870, and the Hayden campaign of 1871. The culmination of these journeys was action by Congress. In 1872, Yellowstone National Park, which included the southern fringe of the Absaroka-Beartooth, was preserved as the world's first national park.

The floodgates were now open to the upper Yellowstone. Because the lower Yellowstone was still closed by the natives, traffic to the national park entered by way of Bozeman and Paradise Valley. F.V. Hayden made a second expedition to the thermal region in 1872, this time accompanied by William Blackmore, an English entrepreneur who had extensive holdings in the Sangre de Cristo range of Colorado and New Mexico. The pair visited the fledgling mining camp of Clarks Fork, later to be named Cooke City. Blackmore's diary of the trip mentions a visit to Crow Agency near present-day Livingston. There, he observed a Crow leader named Bear Tooth.

White settlement at the "bend of the river" got started in 1872 when Amos Benson erected a cabin. Benson's Landing, a notorious trading post and den of iniquity, was succeeded by the more civilized community of Livingston, founded by the Northern Pacific Railroad in 1883.

The location of Crow Agency on Mission Creek near Livingston was ideal for the merchants of Bozeman, but virtually no one else. It was on the extreme western edge of the Crow territory and was a poor link between the natives and the U.S. government. But it provided Bozeman merchants with a golden opportunity for graft and corruption.

By 1875, an investigation revealed widespread organized crime that extended to the office of Secretary of the Interior Columbus Delano. Bozeman merchants, among them the pioneer Nelson Story, made fortunes selling goods to the government, which distributed them to the natives under the terms of the treaties. The merchants were paid in excess of their due—both the Indians and the U.S. government were cheated. Kickbacks to government agents perpetuated the graft.

But greed was the undoing of the scheme. Columbus Delano, found guilty of negligence and incompetence, was forced from office. Crow Agency was moved to the Stillwater. The Bozeman merchants became prominent citizens and philanthropists.

The late 1870s saw the end of the conflicts between whites and Native Americans, and the end of several centuries of native domination of the Yellowstone country. In the spring of 1876, the army began to close in, after several years of reluctance to face the Sioux head on. The advance was hasty and ill-managed, however, and Lt. Col. George A. Custer paid the price on the Little Bighorn. In the winter of 1876-77, Col. Nelson A. Miles subdued the warring Sioux by taking advantage of the cold weather.

Eighteen seventy-seven saw the flight of the Nez Perce. Oppression of this tribe in eastern Washington and northern Idaho led several bands to attempt to seek refuge in Canada. Their flight, respected today for its cunning, resourcefulness, and ethics, passed the southern edge of the Beartooth. After leaving Idaho and surviving an attempted massacre (now called a battle) in the Big Hole valley, the Nez Perce passed through Yellowstone National Park, leaving the eastern boundary of the park by an unknown route, and reaching the plains through the Clarks Fork valley.

Unsubstantiated reports claim that the Nez Perce visited Cooke City, burned the smelter, and stole gold and lead bullion, which were used to make bullets. It's a romantic story, but there is no evidence to support it No newspaper of the time (the closest was the *Avant Courier,* published in Bozeman) mentions such a raid. It's conceivable that a small raiding party entered the mining camp, just as one had ventured down the Yellowstone River to a point below present-day Gardiner, where a ranch was razed and a man killed. However, it was the policy of the Nez Perce leadership to avoid contact with whites. The resident miners may have fabricated the story in later attempts to explain the inactivity of the operation.

With the defeat of the natives, the Beartooth floodgates were opened to settlers and prospectors, even though no treaty had changed the legal ownership of the countryside. Claims were staked at Crevasse, at Independence, at Solomon City, and at hundreds of other long-forgotten nooks in the mountains. In 1880, a treaty with the natives was finally signed, but it wasn't ratified until 1882. By then, the Northern Pacific Railroad was creeping across the prairie and into the valley of the Yellowstone.

By 1883, real civilization had arrived in the Yellowstone Valley. The railroad was completed and numerous towns had sprung up along its route: Billings, Columbus, Big Timber, and Livingston. The Park Branch Northern Pacific rail line was built from Livingston to Cinnabar, near Yellowstone National Park.

A quirk of fate is responsible for the ownership pattern in the Absaroka-Beartooth of today. When the Northern Pacific Railroad was chartered by Congress, a land grant of several sections on either side of the line was made as an incentive and a subsidy. The construction of the line was financed in part by the sale of some of these lands. The checkerboard ownership pattern that resulted is evident in the Crazy Mountains to the north and the Gallatin Range to the west. The Absaroka-Beartooth is virtually a solid block of federal land, however. At the time of the land grant to the railroad, the Absaroka-Beartooth was legally owned by the Crows. With the treaty of 1882, this land was ceded to the U.S. government. The result was solid federal ownership and the opportunity for coherent land management, including wilderness protection, without the problem of mixed ownership.

After 1880, the dominant economic activity in the Absaroka-Beartooth was mining. Smelters were constructed, men were employed, ore was shipped, and fortunes were made and lost. Mining camps were established at Nye, Solomon City, Lake City, Independence, Contact, Cooke City, Jardine, and Crevasse. After the turn of the century, however, things had quieted considerably, due, in part, to the silver crash of 1897. The dreams continued, but few were realized.

After 1900, the economy of the region stabilized. Ranching, tourism, logging, and retailing complemented mining in an economic pattern that continues today. The mining dreams have not died, however. Like the phoenix, mines in the Stillwater Complex and at Jardine have risen from the ashes of the past.

RAILROADS

With the Louisiana Purchase and the acquisition of the Oregon Territory, the United States spanned the North American continent and the idea of a transcontinental railroad was a natural

Autumn in the Beartooth.

one. As early as 1834 a railroad from New York City to the Columbia River was publicly advocated. While the concept of such a railroad was not disputed, the route of the line was. At least three different routes were promoted: northern, central, and southern.

In 1864, after decades of bickering, jockeying, and dispute, Congress passed and President Lincoln signed a bill that chartered the Northern Pacific Railroad and granted a land subsidy estimated at 60 million acres. For the many railroads conceived in the late 1800s, the acquisition of congressional charter was only one step taken toward realization. Several chartered lines never left the station for failure to achieve the most important step—financing.

The land grant was insufficient to get the Northern Pacific under construction, so the railroad's promoters returned to Congress to request more time and a subsidy, similar to that granted to both the Union Pacific and the Central Pacific. But Congress balked. In 1869 the company gave up on a federal subsidy and approached the banking house of Jay Cooke, who sent engineer W. Milnor Roberts to examine the route and estimate costs. Roberts returned with a favorable report. An agreement was consummated in 1870, giving Cooke control of the company and prospects for handsome profits in return for the financing needed to get the line under construction. Congress authorized the company to mortgage its land grant and, in a ceremony at Carlton, Minnesota, on February 15, 1870, ground was broken.

While crews laid track across the prairie, Roberts planned a route over the mountains. In 1871, headquartered in Helena, aided by twenty-five engineers, and escorted by seven companies of infantry to protect them from the hostile Sioux, Roberts surveyed the Yellowstone Valley. Meanwhile, Jay Cooke was conducting an extensive public relations campaign to sell the railroad's bonds. Sales lagged, however, and by late 1872 the board of directors was informed that it must take loans on the personal credit of its members in order to raise money. In May of 1873, Cooke tightened the screws by reducing the amount of bonds he agreed to issue and increasing the interest rate.

Cooke himself was in trouble. In September of 1873, the New York house of Jay Cooke failed during the nation's worst financial panic since 1837. Cooke's Philadelphia house immediately suspended operations and several other brokerage houses closed, as did the New York Stock Exchange and the Gold Exchange. While the economic debris settled, Cooke was blamed for

the panic and his failure was laid at the feet of the Northern Pacific Railroad. In 1875, it went into receivership.

The 1876 Montana territorial legislature, anxious to improve access to the region, drafted a referendum to grant the NP $3.5 million in bonding authority conditioned upon construction of the line from Bismarck to Bozeman. The proposal was defeated in the popular election by a narrow margin.

A reorganization plan for the railroad was proposed by a group headed by Frederick Billings, who became president of the company in 1879. But in 1880, the drama was entered by Henry Villard, owner of the Oregon Railway and Navigation Company, which had been negotiating west coast routes and other issues with the NP. Unable to reach agreements, Villard went after the company. Financed by a "blind pool," through which investors backed him to do whatever he wanted, he began buying Northern Pacific stock. With the aid of litigation, he took control. By 1881, Billings had lost power and Villard managed the company during the final construction phase. The main line was completed under his leadership, but financial woes forced him to resign the presidency of the company in 1884.

Construction proceeded west from Glendive in July of 1881 and reached present-day Livingston seventeen months later. On November 27, 1882, the track reached the last crossing of the Yellowstone, just east of Livingston. Train service between Billings and Livingston began January 15, 1883, when President Grant attended the golden spike ceremony at Gold Creek, Montana. The Northern Pacific, nineteen years after its charter was granted, was finally a transcontinental railroad.

In addition to the main line, the NP built many branches, two of which provided better access to

the Beartooth country. In 1881, Billings, Villard, and others including Wilbur Fisk Sanders and A.M. Holter of Montana, incorporated the Rocky Mountain Rail Road of Montana for the purpose of building a line to Yellowstone National Park. The Northern Pacific, which had supported protection of the park in 1872, was not about to lose its advantage. It surveyed two routes, one up the Yellowstone River to the park's northern entrance, the other up the West Gallatin River. The Yellowstone River location was selected.

The construction contract was let in March of 1883 and by late summer the line was completed to Cinnabar, four miles north of Gardiner, where a land ownership dispute halted further progress. On June 20, 1884, regular passenger service began between Livingston and Cinnabar. It wasn't until 1903 that the line could be completed to Gardiner.

In 1886, entrepreneurs not associated with the NP organized the Rocky Fork and Cooke City Railway, proposing a line that would extend from the NP road near Billings to the Red Lodge coal fields, then to Cooke City. Permission to cross the Crow Reservation was received in March of 1887, and in July, the NP approved a traffic agreement. Surveys began in April of 1887 and by October a contractor was grading a mile a day. But just as work was nearing completion, money ran out.

In August of 1888, the Billings, Clark's Fork and Cooke City Railroad appeared, also with permission to cross the reservation. It announced it would complete the line to Cooke City by July 1889. Aroused by the competition, S.T. Hauser and other NP interests purchased the Rocky Fork and Cooke City Railway and extended it to Red Lodge by April. In 1890, the NP acquired the line.

The extension of rail service to Cooke City

Above: *The Mirror Lake area of the north-central Beartooth.*
Top: *Scars of past mining activity on Lulu Pass.*

Above: *Lake Plateau in the upper Stillwater River drainage.*

Facing page: *Cooke City in its winter clothes.*

never advanced beyond the stages of dreaming and politics. Perhaps it has been the fate of this community to epitomize the isolation of the Beartooth Mountains. Since the discovery of mineral deposits in the area over a century ago, Cooke City has lacked the transportation access to make the town prosper. Not that efforts weren't made.

The town took its name from the Jay Cooke family, which, in 1880, invested in a local mining venture. But the mine wasn't developed and hopes for a railroad withered, as did the later intentions of the Rocky Fork and Cooke City Railway and the Clark's Fork and Cooke City Railroad later in the 1880s, not to mention the efforts of others to breach Yellowstone National Park with a Cooke City railroad from Gardiner.

After the Park Branch had been completed from Livingston to Cinnabar in 1883, promoters, seeing an opportunity to extend the line to the New World Mining District at Cooke City, advanced a bill in Congress to delete the necessary lands from the national park. This bold initiative passed the U.S. House, but was killed in the Senate due to the efforts of Senator George Vest of Missouri and his conservationist constituency motivated by George Bird Grinnell, editor of *Forest and Stream* magazine. A short-lived boom occurred when a Livingston telegraph operator, incorrectly announcing the passage of the measure, prompted a rush of speculation.

Undaunted, a group of Cooke City prospectors and Livingston and Bozeman businessmen raised $1,500 in 1891 to send Sigmund Deutch to Washington D.C. to lobby Congress for a railroad. Deutch's energies and Montana's money, however, were squandered on booze and entertainment. In January of 1884, George Huston of Cooke City and some associates incorporated the Bullion Railroad Company. Its purpose was to construct a line from Cinnabar, through Yellowstone National Park, to Cooke City.

In 1883, articles of incorporation were filed in Cheyenne, Wyoming for Wyoming, Yellowstone Park and Pacific Railroad, one of whose incorporators was L. DuPont, the explosives manufacturer. The company hoped to build an extensive railroad system in Montana, Wyoming, and adjacent territories. All of these efforts to connect Cooke City with the rest of the world failed. It remains almost as isolated today as it was at the turn of the 20th century. Even the Park Branch line to Gardiner has been discontinued.

JAY COOKE

Jay Cooke was a man who thought big. Although of modest roots, he rose to prominence in financial circles and underwrote such ambitious ventures as the Civil War and the Northern Pacific Railroad.

As financier of the Northern Pacific, Cooke played an important role in the settlement of the upper Yellowstone region, including the Beartooth Mountains and their surroundings. Cooke also left his name on the map of Beartooth. Cooke City was named for him in hopes that he would bring the community the railroad it needed for mining development. But the railroad never materialized, the mines never paid off, and Cooke apparently never visited his namesake.

Despite a generous land grant, the financing and construction of the NP was an agonizing affair that took almost twenty years. Jay Cooke had been approached by the company several times in the 1860s, but he had shown no interest in the project. But in 1869, things had changed; Cooke suddenly became interested in railroads because of the decline in government securities. He agreed to underwrite the railroad. His conditions were severe, however; in exchange for financing, he demanded virtual control of the corporation as well as the promise of handsome profit.

Despite his best efforts, Cooke's sale of bonds was insufficient and the first segments of the railroad failed to generate as much revenue as was needed. Overextended and in serious trouble, Cooke could not withstand the Panic of 1873—he declared bankruptcy. It was left to Henry Villard, the brilliant German rail tycoon, to finish the NP.

As for Cooke, he was down, but not out. Released from bankruptcy in 1876, he looked for a way to recoup his fortune. He found it in mining speculation, an area of investment he had previously shunned. For a $3,000 investment in an option in the Horn Silver Mine in Utah, Cooke eventually netted over a million. By 1879, he was once again a millionaire.

The secret of Cooke's success in the Utah venture, in addition to relying on the advice of expert lawyers and engineers, was his ability to persuade the Union Pacific Railroad to build a line to the mine. Though he was virtually broke, his connections, his reputation, and his personality were able to accomplish the task.

After the success of the Horn Silver Mine, Cooke was deluged with requests to bring railroads to other stranded but promising mining districts. Among them was the Clarks Fork Mining District, high in the Beartooth Mountains near Yellowstone National Park and cut off from prosperity by the lack of good transportation.

The showpiece of the mining district was the Great Republic Mine, an outcropping ledge just south of present-day Cooke City that was probably discovered in 1872 by Bart Henderson and his colleagues and officially discovered by George Huston, S.T. Morrow, and Taswell Woody. The claim was relocated in 1875 by Huston, F.D. Pease, and C.W. Hoffman. Pease was the agent at Crow Agency on Mission Creek and Hoffman was the post trader at Fort Ellis near Bozeman. In May of 1879, Hoffman acquired Pease's interest in the claim.

Both Huston and Hoffman were schemers who recognized that their best hope of making money from the Great Republic was to interest someone else in buying it. They found their man in Judge John T. Lynch, postmaster of Salt Lake City, Territory of Utah. Lynch was connected, by way of his father-in-law Alexander Majors, to the Jay Cooke people in Philadelphia.

The connection to Lynch was made through Maj. James Brisbin, commander at Fort Ellis. A crony of Hoffman's, Brisbin claimed he had visited the ledge at the Great Republic and that, among other things, the ore would be worth $75,000,000. Later, doubt was cast on Brisbin's report; he hadn't been within forty miles of the district.

Judge Lynch was sufficiently intrigued with the Great Republic that he sent his associate Thomas W. Bates to investigate, with instructions to secure a bond on the mine if Brisbin's statements held up. Bates returned to Salt Lake City with the bond in hand, purchased for the option price of $3,000. The option entitled the speculators to investigate further and, if they liked what they saw, acquire the property for a total of $47,500.

Lynch, Bates, and their partner Joseph Jorgenson of Philadelphia immediately engaged the services of Alexander Majors, Lynch's father-in-law, to sell the mine. Majors wasted no time in interesting Jay Cooke, Jr. and Frank Thomson in the property. A new company was formed with Lynch, Bates, and Jorgenson holding $1/24$ interests each. Others involved included Jay Cooke, Jr. ($2/24$), Jay Cooke ($2/24$), John M. Butler, Jay Cooke's son-in-law and confidant ($2/24$), and Alex Majors ($2/24$). Thomson and others held the remaining shares. An additional $7,000 was pledged for further investigation of the mine. The option was valid until July 1, 1880 (later extended to August 1, due to the late snows in the mountains).

In typical Jay Cooke fashion, a team of engineers and lawyers, headed by John Butler, was dispatched for the Clarks Fork Mining District in the spring of 1880. The chief engineer was E.Y. Eltonhead of Philadelphia.

The miners of the district were ecstatic. Now they could all be rich, thanks to the soon-to-be-constructed railroad that would convert their dreams to reality. A townsite was laid out and at a meeting on June 8, the group unanimously selected a name: Cooke City. The community was spruced up for the first time in anticipation of the visit from the representatives of Jay Cooke.

But the visit was disappointing for all. The lawyers couldn't show clear title to the property because the district was on the Crow Indian reservation. A treaty ceding the Absaroka-Beartooth to the United States was negotiated that year but had not yet been ratified by Congress (and would not be until 1882).

Eltonhead and his engineers found the claims of Hoffman, Huston, Brisbin, Lynch, and Bates to be wildly exaggerated. An eighty-mile railroad would be needed and no justification could be found for the nearly $1 million in development costs. The town of Cooke City suffered another in a long and continuing series of disappointments. In the end, more money was made at Cooke City through mining speculation than from mining.

In the summer of 1891, Jay Cooke and his family finally rode the Northern Pacific railroad all the way to the west coast. Stopping for a few days in Yellowstone National Park, they enjoyed the scenic wonders that Cooke and the railroad had helped set aside in 1872 as the world's first national preserve. But they apparently didn't visit Cooke City.

Jim Bridger

Few men played as important a role in the opening of the mountain west as Jim Bridger. His legend is a fascinating blend of fact and fancy, enhanced by Bridger's penchant for spinning imaginative yarns. When the man beneath the myth is stripped of the fiction, however, there remains an integral figure in Rocky Mountain history. Bridger's travels took him to the Beartooth at a time when few whites had ventured into this ruggedly wild and remote sanctuary.

Bridger was born in 1804, the year in which Lewis and Clark departed St. Louis, en route to the Pacific Northwest. By the time Bridger was a young man, the Rocky Mountains were still largely unexplored. John Colter, who left Lewis and Clark in 1806, was perhaps the only white man who had previously visited the country at the headwaters of the Yellowstone, Snake, and Green rivers.

In 1825, at the age of twenty-one, Bridger joined the service of Gen. William H. Ashley as a contract trapper, assigned to the upper Bighorn. Alone, on a sturdy raft of lashed cottonwood logs, he successfully navigated the Bighorn Canyon, known then as Bad Pass. The exploit allegedly earned him the enduring respect of the natives who expressed their admiration by confiding in Bridger much of their knowledge of the surrounding geography. They confirmed that the French (the Verendrye brothers) had visited the Yellowstone long ago; they confirmed the existence of thermal activity in the region now known as Yellowstone National Park; and they confirmed what had been theorized for decades—the Yellowstone, the Columbia (Snake), and the Colorado (Green) rivers head near each other. Armed with new insights into the lay of the land, Bridger led a group of trappers around the protected plateau of the upper Yellowstone.

In the winter of 1835-36, Bridger organized a company of about 240 trappers that met on the north shore of Yellowstone Lake. They branched out in several directions, some undoubtedly into the Hellroaring, Slough Creek, Boulder, and Stillwater drainages of the Beartooth, although history holds no records of these routes. Bridger led the main party down the Yellowstone River, through the Second Canyon (later, Yankee Jim's), Paradise Valley, and the First Canyon. At the mouth of the Twenty-five Yard River (today's Shields), the various factions of the Yellowstone Lake party reunited.

After traveling across the northern foothills of the Beartooth, a second reunion was convened at Rocky Fork (Rock Creek) near present-day Red Lodge. From there, the group went east to Pryor Creek, then south to the Wind River.

By 1838, Jim Bridger had become the top-ranking mountain man and hosted that year's rendezvous, held on the Wind River. Bridger spent the next several years in the lower Green River, trapping and trading. He established Fort Bridger and underwent a period of relative domestication.

In 1859, Bridger was employed by Captain William F. Raynolds to guide his party to the headwaters of the Yellowstone River in search of the fabled thermal features. (Another notable member of that expedition was Dr. F.V. Hayden, who was early in his career but destined to become one of the nation's premier scientific explorers.) Despite Bridger's fifteen-year absence from the region, his memory was consistent with the landscape. But late-lying snows and Raynolds' adherence to an exacting schedule (and perhaps his failure to heed Bridger's advice) thwarted attempts to penetrate the Yellowstone Plateau. The best routes, up Pacific Creek to the Thoroughfare and up the Madison to the geyser basin, were bypassed.

In the early 1860s, Montana's mineral resources were yet untapped, but rumors of their wealth

Above: *Line Creek on the Line Creek Plateau.*
Right: *Rough Lake.*

flourished. The prospectors who discovered the bonanzas at Bannack and Alder Gulch had entered the country by way of Utah; the Crow and Sioux had made travel into the Yellowstone a perilous endeavor. In the fall of 1863, John Bozeman had established a route north of the Bighorn Mountains into the heart of Native American country. Bridger, then sixty years old, was under contract with the Army at Fort Laramie (as a consulting expert on native peoples). Bridger, far more knowledgeable of the topography than the upstart Bozeman, was not to be outdone. He advocated a shorter, easier, and safer route to the south of the Bighorns. Though Bridger's route—known as the "Bridger Cutoff"—had mea-

ger forage for pack stock, it was 100 miles shorter than the Bozeman Trail and it avoided the hostile Sioux.

In April of 1864, a band of would-be miners from Denver gathered at Fort Laramie; their destination—the gold fields of Montana. Their choices were three. They could follow the established and well-traveled Oregon Trail to Fort Hall (Idaho), then cross Monida Pass into Montana. They could risk their scalps on the Bozeman Trail. Or they could follow Bridger. They chose the latter. On April 30, 1864, Bridger obtained a leave of absence from the army and departed Ft. Laramie with some 300 people in 62 wagons.

By July 4, when they reached the Yellowstone

The Beartooth Range History

Map by Ed Madej

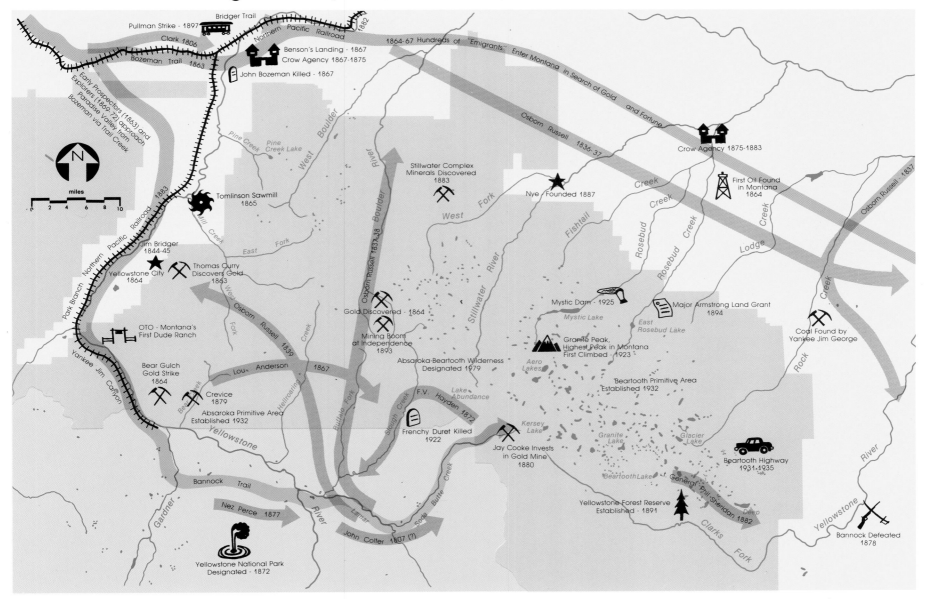

Pullman Strike - 1897

Bridger Trail

Clark 1806

Bozeman Trail 1863

Northern Pacific Railroad 1882

1864-67 Hundreds of "Emigrants" Enter Montana in Search of Gold and Fortune

Benson's Landing - 1867
Crow Agency 1867-1875

John Bozeman Killed - 1867

Early Prospectors (1863) and Explorers (1869-72) approach Paradise Valley from Bozeman via Trail Creek

Osborn Russell 1836-37

Crow Agency 1875-1883

Pine Creek

Pine Creek Lake

West Boulder

Osborn Russell - 1837

First Oil Found in Montana 1864

miles
0 2 4 6 8 10

Tomlinson Sawmill 1865

Stillwater Complex Minerals Discovered 1883

Nye - Founded 1887

East Fork

West Fork

Boulder River

Fishtail Creek

Rosebud Creek

Rosebud Creek

Lodge Creek

Northern Pacific Railroad 1883

Park Branch

Jim Bridger 1844-45

Mill Creek

Yellowstone City 1864

Thomas Curry Discovers Gold 1863

Gold Discovered - 1864

Mystic Dam - 1925

Mystic Lake

Major Armstrong Land Grant 1894

East Rosebud Lake

Coal Found by Yankee Jim George

OTO - Montana's First Dude Ranch

West Fork

Osborn Russell 1839

Mining Boom at Independence 1893

Granite Peak, Highest Peak in Montana First Climbed - 1923

Aero Lakes

Beartooth Primitive Area Established 1932

Rock Creek

Yankee Jim Canyon

Bear Creek

Bear Gulch Gold Strike 1864

Lou Anderson 1867

Crevice 1879

Absaroka-Beartooth Wilderness Designated 1979

Lake Abundance

Granite Lake

Glacier Lake

Absaroka Primitive Area Established 1932

Helroaring Creek

Yellowstone

Buffalo Fork

Slough Creek

F.V. Hayden 1872

Frenchy Duret Killed 1922

Kersey Lake

Beartooth Highway 1931-1935

Bannock Trail

Nez Perce 1877

Jay Cooke Invests in Gold Mine 1880

Soda Butte Creek

Beartooth Lake

Gen. Phil Sheridan 1882

Yellowstone Forest Reserve Established - 1891

Deep Lake

Clarks Fork

Yellowstone River

Gardner

River

Lamar

John Colter 1807 (?)

Yellowstone National Park Designated - 1872

Bannock Defeated 1878

Major Trails and Travel Routes

Routes of Early Explorers

Historic Sites

River, Bridger's assemblage had been caught and joined by several parties. His flock now numbered almost a thousand. Near the mouth of the Shields River, the train was met by Thomas Curry, the discoverer of gold at Emigrant Gulch. Curry recruited several men, among them David Shorthill, to accompany him to the gulch. Bridger led the balance of the party up the Shields River, over Bridger Pass, into the Gallatin valley, and on to Virginia City, arriving on July 12. Bozeman's train, in something of a race, crossed Bozeman Pass and entered the Gallatin valley before Bridger and his entourage.

A year later, both Bridger and Bozeman were in the employ of N.P. Langford's Missouri River and Rocky Mountain Wagon Road, conducting emigrant trains to Montana from Fort Laramie.

David Shorthill and his colleagues, having left the Bridger train at the mouth of the Shields River, struck paydirt at Emigrant Gulch. Near the mouth of the gulch, they observed a tree with a ring of elk antlers arranged around the base. Later, Jim Bridger claimed to have left them there some 25 years earlier. It could have been on his trip down the Yellowstone in the winter of 1835-36.

Bannock Trail

The Bannock tribe occupied southeastern Idaho, where streams teemed with trout and the Snake River plain was well stocked with bison. But in the late 1830s, when the buffalo dramatically (and inexplicably) disappeared, the Bannocks were forced either to move to a buffalo-rich location elsewhere, thus risking intertribal conflict, or to ameliorate a profound dependence on the buffalo. A compromise between these extremes was adopted when the tribe opted to stage annual migrations to the plains to the east where buffalo were still plentiful.

The decision to travel to the plains involved consideration of alternative routes. They could go north to the Yellowstone, or as far as the forks of the Missouri. They could venture south and east toward the Platte. Or they could go more or less straight east through either Jackson Hole or the Yellowstone hot springs region. Their choice was largely determined by intertribal politics. Through the thermal region, they could cross lands inhabited by the passive Sheepeaters and afford maximum safety to women and children.

Starting at Camas Prairie, the ancestral camps of the Bannocks in southeastern Idaho, the Bannock Trail crossed Targhee Pass, entered the Madison River area of what is now the park, crossed the Yellowstone River near Tower Falls, and followed the Lamar River to its confluence with Soda Butte Creek, skirting the southern fringe of the Absaroka-Beartooth. At Soda Butte Creek, the trail branched. The easiest route, and the one used the most in the early years, ascended Soda Butte Creek and passed over the gentle divide to the Clarks Fork River near today's Cooke City.

Upon the establishment of the New World Mining District at Cooke City in about 1870, the Bannocks altered their route to avoid the mining camp. This route climbed the open ridge between Miller and Calfee creeks, passed over the divide near Canoe Lake, and descended to the plains via Crandall Creek and the Clarks Fork.

The Bannock Trail had other branches, used variously for side trips, intertribal trade junkets, and raiding missions. One stem paralleled the Yellowstone River through the Paradise Valley; another penetrated the high Absaroka country to the Boulder River via Slough Creek. Other

offshoots entered the Madison, Gallatin, and Shoshone valleys.

For many years the annual migration was successful. The seasonal treks brought abundant protein into the Bannock diet and engendered trade opportunities with other tribes. By the mid-1800s, however, when discoveries of gold and other minerals in Idaho and southwestern Montana led to a U.S. policy of reservations and treaties enforced by the army, the fortunes of the Bannocks began to ebb.

The Bannocks assigned to the Fort Hall reservation were no less hostile to the idea of confined residency than any other tribes suddenly governed by whites. In 1878, after a period of unrest resulting from dissatisfaction with living conditions, violence erupted. Among the many frays between the Bannocks and the whites was one in the Beartooth region.

On August 27, 1878, a band of Bannocks, later described as hostile, had a skirmish with a surveying party near Henry's Lake. The next day, the same band clashed with an army troop. The Bannocks were then forced to flee, by what turned out to be essentially the same route as the Nez Perce had taken the previous year.

In the meantime, Col. Nelson A. Miles, already renowned for his decisive and effective action in subduing the Sioux in the winter of 1876-77 and catching the Nez Perce in the fall of 1877, sought respite from the business of war and prepared for a holiday in Yellowstone National Park with his family. He was escorted on his vacation by two small companies of mounted infantry.

Arriving at Crow Agency on the Stillwater River on August 29, 1878, he learned of the approaching Bannocks from 1st Lt. William P. Clark, who had encountered them while ascending the Stillwater River toward Pilot Peak. Miles took steps to intercept the runaways.

After sending his family to Ft. Ellis, Miles dispatched part of his force, under 2nd Lt. Hobart K. Bailey, to the Boulder River where they took up a position near the Natural Bridge. Miles, along with Capt. Andrew Bennett, the remaining company of infantry, about seventy-five Crow warriors, and a cannon, started for the Clarks Fork. He found the Bannocks camped at the mouth of a stream on the southern flank of the Beartooth Plateau. The colonel attacked immediately and, after three hours of fighting, the Bannocks were beaten: eleven were killed and thirty-two captured. Those Bannocks who escaped were taken into custody a few weeks later near the Tongue River. Capt. Bennett and Little Rock, a Frenchman who had joined the Crows as an interpreter, were Miles' only casualties.

Finn Burnett, a frontiersman who came upon the scene the following day, described the battleground:

"The thickets had been blown to bits by cannon shots, and the dead bodies of squaws and papooses lay with the remains of Bannock warriors amid the wreckage…The path along which the Bannock fled was still slippery with blood.…"

To the victors go the spoils and the honors. The Bannocks, fleeing the oppression of the reservation, provided few spoils beyond the 200 horses and mules won by Miles and given to the Crows. But the stream at the site of the battle was named for Captain Bennett and its upstream neighbor for Little Rock, the casualties of the victorious army. Today Bennett and Littlerock creeks bathe the Beartooth Plateau in their honor. The defeated Bannocks were returned to Fort Hall, never again to make their annual trek to the plains.

LOST CITIES OF THE ABSAROKA-BEARTOOTH

A glance at Rand-McNally's 1893 *New Business Atlas Map of Montana* is startling on two counts. First, it shows Sweet Grass County, which wasn't created until 1895. Second, it locates a town (or place) called Maxwell on the Buffalo Fork, a tributary of Slough Creek, which drains the south slopes of the Absaroka-Mountains, north of Yellowstone National Park. Sweet Grass County could have been a sparkle in the eye of a politician or cartographer. Or the map could have been misdated. However, these and similar explanations fail to account for the appearance of Maxwell.

A check of postal records reveals that there was indeed a post office in Park County in a place called Maxwell for a few months in 1893, with a postmaster named Joel M. Gaylor. When the office was discontinued in November of 1893, the mail was routed to Independence, near the head of the Main Boulder River and a scant 20 miles from the location shown by Rand-McNally for Maxwell. Thus, postal records tend to substantiate at least the general location of such a community.

Exactly where was Maxwell? After whom was it named? Who lived there? Why were they there?

No physical evidence of a onetime community in Buffalo Fork can be found. No roads, no abandoned mines, no signs of timber cutting, no dilapidated buildings, not even any foundations. In the 1920s, the area around Maxwell was included in the Absaroka Primitive Area; it is now in the heart of the Absaroka-Beartooth Wilderness. Only wild forested country exists where Maxwell might have been.

As in many other places in the wilderness, an occasional remnant of an old cabin can be found—presumably occupied by trappers or prospectors. But never are several found together; in total, there are too few to envision enough demand for mail to justify a post office. Paying minerals have never been found in Buffalo Fork, and there have never been enough beaver or marten to support more than a couple of trappers.

Perplexingly, the community of Maxwell has faded from the memories of our culture in 100 years. Its name appears nowhere in the historical literature, other than the 1893 map and the postal records. Local historians have never heard of it, nor have people who have lived in Gardiner and Cooke City for eighty years.

A second mystery involves the long-forgotten community of Hawkwood, shown on the 1897 map of the General Land Office and 1902 maps published by George F. Cram and Hibbard and Van Hook. On all three maps the exact location is unclear; Hawkwood lies west of Contact on the Boulder River, north of Mount Cowen, and east of the Yellowstone River. According to postal records, a post office was established in 1903, after which time the mail was sent to Bruffey's, now the Triangle Seven ranch at the confluence of Mission and Little Mission creeks, east of Livingston. The location of Hawkwood was probably on the West Boulder, about ten miles above McLeod. The West Boulder was settled by early pioneers, so Hawkwood's past isn't as mysterious as that of Maxwell. It is perplexing, though, that an entire community can almost disappear from our cultural memory in less than a century.

Many other communities have blossomed briefly on the periphery of the Absaroka-Beartooth, many of them in Paradise Valley. Among them: Hayden, Richland, Riverside, Brisbin, Chicory, Daileys, Sphinx, Herron, Fridley, and Yellowstone City.

RUDYARD KIPLING MEETS

YANKEE JIM

Rudyard Kipling rightfully fancied himself quite a storyteller, but he met his match, and more, in "Yankee Jim" George. In 1889, Kipling, then twenty-four years old, returned to England from the Orient by way of the United States. Traveling by train, he took a side trip to Yellowstone National Park and stopped en route to fish for trout in the white water of the canyon now known as Yankee Jim. Of his encounter with Jim, Kipling wrote in *From Sea to Sea* (New York: Doubleday and McClure Company, 1899):

"They halted the train at the head of a narrow valley, and I leaped literally into the arms of Yankee Jim, sole owner of a log hut, an indefinite amount of hay-ground, and constructor of twenty-seven miles of wagon-road over which he held toll right. There was the hut—the river fifty yards away, and the polished line of metals that disappeared round a bluff. That was all. The railway added the finishing touch to the already complete loneliness of the place. Yankee Jim was a picturesque old man with a talent for yarns that Ananias might have envied. It seemed to me, presumptuous in my ignorance, that I might hold my own with the old-timer if I judiciously painted up a few lies gathered in the course of my wandering. Yankee Jim saw every one of my tales and went fifty better on the spot. He dealt in bears and natives—never less than twenty of each; had known the Yellowstone country for years, and bore upon his body marks of Indian arrows; and his eyes had seen a squaw of the Crows burned alive at the stake. He said she screamed considerable."

RESORTS

From the first occupation of the Beartooth region by white people, its beauty and its wildlife lent themselves to a tourist industry. The first tourists were probably military men who, after the Civil War and the Indian campaigns, turned their energies to hunting and wildlife preservation. Many of them were interested in Yellowstone National Park and hunted in its surrounding areas. By the late 1800s, local hunters and former trappers had established themselves as skilled and reliable hunting guides.

One of those guides was Dick Randall, who, as a young man in search of adventure, got a job with George Wakefield's stage line in Yellowstone National Park in 1887. Randall, a "good mixer," met affluent tourists in the summer, establishing contacts that he parlayed into a thriving fall hunt-

GEORGE ROBBINS

MICHAEL S. SAMPLE

Above: Rising trout dimple the surface of Island Lake.
Left: Sawtooth Mountain.

Facing page, left top: South face of Granite Peak, viewed from Skytop Lakes.
Left bottom: Camp Sawtooth.
Right: McLaren Mine near Cooke City.

ing business in the Hellroaring country north of the park and in Jackson Hole south of the park.

Randall yearned for a permanent headquarters, and in 1898 he bought squatters rights to a claim on Cedar Creek, north of Gardiner where he had been wintering his horses for several years. This, the OTO Ranch, became Montana's first dude ranch. Starting with a one-room bunkhouse and a spare room on the family ranch house, the spread grew to include a lodge and several cabins.

In 1910 Randall expanded his thriving business to a wilderness setting, on Hellroaring Creek, in the meadow at the mouth of Horse Creek. There, he built log cabin accommodations for sixteen people as well as a kitchen and a dining room. The thirty-five-mile ride from the OTO was made in two days.

In 1914, Randall built a large T-shaped lodge at the OTO and began to make annual winter trips to the east coast to promote his popular operation. His largest pack trip, a 1927 Sierra Club outing of 173 people, required a crew of forty, and 200 head of stock. The business was largely a product of his personality, however, and after he retired from dude ranching in 1934, the OTO was never the same. After many years as a working cattle ranch, it was acquired successively by Malcolm Forbes, the Church Universal and Triumphant, the Rocky Mountain Elk Foundation, and, finally, the U.S. Forest Service.

In 1913, the Shaw and Powell Camping Company established a series of camps in Yellowstone National Park and one at Cooke City. Transportation was provided by stage coach. From Cooke City, horse trips were conducted to a smaller camp at Goose Lake and on to Grasshopper Glacier.

An early resort on the east side of the Beartooth was Camp Sawtooth, established in an extremely remote canyon on the southeast side of the Pla-

teau. Deep Lake, formed by a landslide in the canyon of Littlerock Creek, is quite inaccessible, but upstream about a mile, in the shadow of Sawtooth Mountain, is a willow-filled meadow through which the creek pleasantly meanders. In 1922, F.I. Johnson got a Forest Service permit and built a grand lodge and several cabins. In addition to regular Saturday night dances and parties at Camp Sawtooth, Johnson guided hunters and fishermen.

Over the years, Camp Sawtooth became difficult to operate and maintain. By 1962, the owners relinquished the permit, unable to meet the terms of the Forest Service and still make a reasonable profit. In 1969, the buildings were razed. All that remains today are the lodge's crumbling stone fireplace, a few foundation traces, and the memories of dancing to fiddle music beneath the crystal-clear sky above the Beartooth Plateau.

Beartooth Lake, near Beartooth Butte, was the site of another early resort. Settlement there dated from at least 1912, when Jim Redfern built a cabin and spent the winter. After the country was overrun with settlers, Redfern, a genuine loner, retired to the wilds of the upper Bitterroot where he had grown up; the Forest Service made a ranger cabin of his domicile.

By the 1920s the camp at Beartooth Lake had become a resort. People came to enjoy the scenery and to fish and hunt. They also came to party. The annual summer dance at Camp Beartooth was famous for miles around.

In 1933, Roy Hicox built the first lodge at Beartooth Lake. By then, the Beartooth Highway was open from Cooke City and people could drive in, dance, drink, and stay overnight in relative comfort. The first automobile traffic arrived at Beartooth Lake in 1932, when Cooke City folks drove, some of them drunk, to the annual dance and party at Beartooth Lake.

In the 1940s H.S. Flatt secured a permit to expand the facilities at Camp Beartooth. He built sixteen cabins, a lodge, and a bathhouse. The Camp soon boasted a photo shop and was the site of the Top-of-the-World store. By the 1960s, however, business had dwindled so much that in 1966 the permit was terminated and most of the buildings were moved to Cooke Pass. In 1967, the Top-of-the-World store was moved to its present location.

Today, Jim Redfern would be appalled with the crowds that visit Beartooth Lake, even in the winter. A contemporary visitor must stretch the imagination to appreciate the solitude that once accompanied the area's beauty.

Many other dude ranches and resorts have come and gone around the Beartooth. Some have thrived, some have faded, and some remain today. Among those that are presently operating are Chico Hot Springs, Beartooth Ranch on the Stillwater River, Aller's Boulder River Ranch, the Snowy Range Ranch on the East Fork of Mill Creek, Hawley Mountain Guest Ranch on the Main Boulder, the Sixty Three Ranch on Mission Creek, the X Bar A on the Boulder, and the Hunter Peak Ranch on the Clarks Fork River. Several other operations have faded: the Lazy Day on the Boulder, the Burnt Leather on the West Boulder, and Corwin Springs.

EAST ROSEBUD LAKE

The canyon of East Rosebud Creek epitomizes the spectacular beauty of the Beartooth. Its soaring cliffs and roaring cascades, part of a topography reminiscent of Yosemite, give cause for some to boast, and some to concede, that this is the most spectacular and beautiful of the Beartooth canyons.

Its cliffs soar to dazzling heights; its cascades

tumble unrestrained from pool to pool over smooth ledges through alpine and subalpine lakes. The creek originates above timberline at one of the few places in the Beartooth where the pass to the high plateau is gentle, not headed by a rugged glacial cirque with impassable walls. Fossil Lake, the remnant of a glacier that failed in its attempt to carve a deep canyon, lies near the summit of what was once known as Pavement Pass. The topography near Fossil Lake is subdued, though the shoreline of the lake is long and torturous.

From Fossil Lake, the East Rosebud flows calmly northeastward, gathering tributaries and speed before reaching Dewey and Twin Outlets lakes. Leaping over Impasse Falls, it then hopscotches a series of jewels: Dugan Lake, Big Park Lake, Lake at Falls, the Rainbow Lakes, Rimrock Lake, Elk Lake, and, finally, East Rosebud Lake. On its descent from the plateau, the East Rosebud is bolstered by several other cascading streams—Granite, Falls, Whirlpool, Arch, Fivemile, and Snow creeks.

Although East Rosebud Lake is several miles upstream from the mouth of the creek's canyon, it marks a transition in the Beartooth landscape. Downstream from the lake, the canyon is less rugged and its sage is reminiscent of the arid prairie and foothills. The lake, formed by an alluvial fan washed into the canyon by Spread Creek, also marks the natural end of the canyon's ascent by motorized transportation. The sharp relief upstream from the lake is a barrier to vehicles, but most motorists find East Rosebud Lake to be a satisfying destination.

One of the first people to reach this conclusion was Major H.J. Armstrong, the Indian Agent at Crow Agency, miles downstream, in the 1880s. Major Armstrong often visited the lake and, after he left his post at Crow Agency under pressure, he resolved to stay. Well enough connected to Congress to acquire a grant of 108 acres at the Lake in 1896, Armstrong built a cabin and grazed horses on the large meadow by the lake.

In 1899, a devastating fire burned several thousand acres and marred the beauty of the once idyllic lake. Discouraged and financially beset, Armstrong sold out in 1905 to a group of Red Lodge bankers. By 1907, the property had settled into the hands of Christian Yegen of Billings and John Chapman of Red Lodge. In 1912 the owners built a lodge, where room and board were available.

To Yegen and his friends, the recreational appeal of East Rosebud Lake was obvious. They resolved to preserve the lake and its surroundings for the enjoyment of their families in such a way that the primitive setting would not be altered. Thus, in 1916, a nonprofit family association was incorporated and began to issue twenty-five-year leases. The association, which continues today, adopted policies that allowed a limited number of cabins and second homes to be built, but restricted development of the lake shore. The scars of the 1899 fire have healed and the lodge no longer provides room and board, but a store is open to the public for vacation essentials.

Some members of the association are fifth-generation visitors to the East Rosebud. Like their ancestors, they share a love for the lake, along with the philosophy of unobtrusive coexistence spawned by Major Armstrong.

FRENCHY DURET

In June of 1922 the Montana press reported the killing of Frenchy Duret, guide, outfitter, hunter, and rancher, by a ferocious grizzly in Slough Creek, just north of the Yellowstone National Park boundary. At the time of his death, the diminutive Duret was said to have killed over 200 grizzlies in his long, colorful career.

Frenchy came into the Slough Creek country in the 1890s, having tried his hand at mining in the Stillwater. In the secluded meadows of Slough Creek that bear his name today, he found an idyllic haven. Slough Creek flows southerly into Yellowstone National Park where it joins the Lamar River. In its headwaters, it is ringed by 10,000-foot mountains and 9,000-foot passes. Thus, the best access to the drainage is up Slough Creek from Yellowstone Park. Frenchy homesteaded the meadow where he operated a ranch and hunted bear and elk.

He also poached in the park. He was known to be devious and was a constant thorn in the side of the Forest Service. The Park Service considered him menace to the wildlife of the park.

Frenchy grew and cut hay on his homesteaded meadow. He fed both elk and cattle, and was frustrated by the unwillingness of the park administration to let him trail his cattle through the national park. His markets were in Cooke City and Gardiner, where he sold meat and hides. Occasionally, he slipped an elk carcass into a shipment of beef.

Naturally, Frenchy was territorial about Slough Creek. In 1897, he wrote a letter to the park superintendent complaining bitterly about poaching in Slough Creek. Someone was encroaching on his turf!

Frenchy thrived, and in 1913, at the age of fifty-two, he took a bride. Jennie McWilliams was ideal for the intrepid Frenchman—she filed on her own homestead in the meadow and built her own cabin. She got along with Frenchy about as well as the bears did.

Frenchy's luck with bears was bound to run out. On June 12, 1922, after checking his traps, he

returned for his rifle, telling Jennie he had caught a large grizzly. He never returned. A search party found his remains the next day. He had apparently crawled a mile and a half, mortally wounded in a titanic struggle won by the bear, which escaped with the trap.

Both the Park Service and the Forest Service saw Frenchy's death as an opportunity to solve a nagging problem. Superintendent Horace Albright interested Sol Guggenheim and Thomas Cochrane (the latter of the J.P. Morgan firm) in the property. In September of 1922, Albright took a party including Cochrane and Jim Anderson (variously described as a ranch manager for the Harrimans' Railroad Ranch in eastern Idaho, a Salt Lake City contractor, and a big game hunter) to inspect Slough Creek. Jennie was prepared to sell the meadow to a group of poachers and tooth hunters for $1,200 but Anderson saved the day on the spot by making an offer they couldn't match. With the condition that the Silvertip Ranch, then owned by the park's chief buffalokeeper Lacombe and Grand Canyon National Park chief ranger Charles Smith, be included, Anderson agreed to pay $13,000.

In 1923, the Bliss family of New York visited Slough Creek and bought Silvertip Ranch and Frenchy's Meadow, retaining "Hellroaring Jim" Anderson as the manager. The Blisses operated the property as a vacation retreat for family and friends for sixty years.

In 1988, the U.S. Forest Service obtained a conservation easement on Frenchy's Meadow. It provides for public access and precludes commercial development or subdivision.

Frenchy Duret played a dominant role in the sad drama of the grizzly bear. He personally killed perhaps as many as exist today in the entire Greater Yellowstone ecosystem. But his meadow, no longer cropped for hay, is wilder today than it was at the turn of the 20th century. Its preservation as wild, open space can provide an anchor in the sea of diminishing habitat for the threatened bear.

STOCKADE

In the Littlerock drainage, between the Beartooth Highway and the Clarks Fork Canyon, is a relic of perhaps the first white occupation of the Beartooth plateau. Known now as the "stockade," it was discovered in 1891 by "Pack Saddle" Ben Greenough, a Red Lodge cowboy who was punching cows for the Dillworth Cattle Company. Familiar with the plateau and knowing that few whites had reason to visit it, Greenough took an interest in the peculiar ruin he found near Leg Lake.

It was roughly oval in shape, measuring about forty by sixty feet. Strategically built in a stand of lodgepole pines, the structure was made of logs, some cut and felled on the spot, others apparently dragged some distance, stacked on one another and woven among the standing lodgepoles. One wall was double; the space between the small logs was filled with rocks. A few of the logs had notches, presumably for the insertion of rifles through the walls.

Many of the structure's logs had crudely cut

Above: Paying respects to Frenchy Duret.
Top: Frenchy's Meadow below Cutoff Mountain.

Facing page: Spring runoff overwhelms East Rosebud Creek. GEORGE WUERTHNER

ends, apparently felled and fitted with primitive tools in the hands of unskilled workers. Other logs had cleanly cut ends, as though they had been trimmed by expert woodsmen using sharp metal tools such as bitted axes.

The stockade appeared to have provided a lengthy occupancy. Charcoal, burned wood, and game animal bones were scattered about. Crude stone fireplaces abutted one wall, and poles indicated the use of bark or hides for shelter.

John K. Rollinson, an early settler in the Sunlight Basin and forest ranger in that district from 1906 to 1913, visited the stockade in 1907. Based on the evidence he saw, Rollinson estimated that the structure was built prior to 1860, dating it to a time when the only white men in the region were trappers who resided principally in the sheltered valleys.

Writing in 1942, Rollinson pondered: "Perhaps some day history will unearth this present mystery of the how, when and why of the old stockade." The old stockade can still be found. Its remains are consistent with the observations of both Greenough and Rollinson. The mystery also remains.

THE MONTANA METEOR

T.C. "Chalk" Benbow of Absarokee, Montana, was a jack of many trades and a master of several. He was a rancher, a farmer, and an inventor, holding patents on an automobile wheel with coil spring spokes, an automatic railroad coupling, and an air brake. He was a prospector and miner who claimed and developed the Benbow chrome mine in the Beartooth's Stillwater Complex.

He was also a pilot. No ordinary pilot, he dreamed of a unique and wonderful mode of flight—the lighter-than-air balloon.

Around the turn of the 20th century, Chalk exhibited a model of his dirigible, powered by an electric motor, in a Red Lodge saloon window. In 1902, Benbow formed the American Aerial Navigation Company to finance his dream—a semirigid dirigible balloon capable of carrying passengers. Within a year, pledges totaling more than $30,000 had been made, though only $5,000 had been collected. This modest start enabled and inspired Benbow to visit the recognized oracle of balloon travel, Dr. Carl Meyer, the country's leading expert on lighter-than-air construction.

Meyer listened to Benbow's vision, studied his plans, then endorsed the idea and agreed to build a prototype. Powered by a four-cylinder, fan-cooled engine, the balloon was christened The Montana Meteor. Its first test flights were conducted in 1903.

The hydrogen-filled Meteor was an elegant craft, enveloped in French silk and covered with twelve coats of Meyer's special varnish. The spindle-shaped gas bag, measuring 74 feet long and 21 feet in diameter, had a capacity of 14,000 cubic feet, producing a lift of more than 900 pounds. The balloon employed a unique rotor comprised of variable pitch blades; the advancing blades collapsed and the retreating blades opened to provide forward thrust.

The announcement of the nation's first air meet, scheduled for the 1904 St. Louis International World's Exposition and timed to coincide with the Democratic National Convention, gave Benbow and his backers an ideal opportunity to exhibit the new airship. Chalk became one of a handful of balloon enthusiasts to vie for the grand prize of $100,000, to go to the fastest ship. To qualify, a balloon had to lap a ten-mile course three times at a minimum average speed of twenty miles an hour. The winner would be the balloon to reach the greatest speed above that.

Benbow's first official run was disappointing—his gas was contaminated and the ship's lift was insufficient. A second run was successful, and the Meteor qualified, along with two other craft, one owned by Dr. Meyer.

In November of 1904, Benbow vied for the grand prize. Starting cautiously, his first competitive flight was modest. The balloon soared to a height of fifty feet and remained aloft for fifteen minutes. Chalk steered the ship in all directions, then slowly descended. Two weeks later, Benbow took the Meteor to 2,000 feet, but had to return prematurely when the gas line developed a leak and the engine lost power.

As a precaution, Benbow added an auxiliary engine. On the next run, the Meteor's anchor snagged and the envelope became hopelessly ensnared in the wire enclosure of the race concourse. Benbow slid safely to the ground, but the accident was fatal for the ship, whose fragile silk skin had been damaged beyond immediate repair.

Benbow retired to Montana to pursue other dreams, but he never lost his love of flight, although The Montana Meteor never flew again. The $100,000 grand prize at St. Louis went unclaimed. The judges had set the performance standards higher than the day's balloons could reach.

MYSTIC LAKE HYDROELECTRIC PLANT

The Absaroka-Beartooth is largely wilderness, due principally to the region's lack of exploitable resources and its harsh winter climate. An anomaly to this condition is the Mystic Lake hydroelectric project, forty-five miles southwest of Columbus, Montana, on West Rosebud Creek.

The canyons of the Beartooth are inviting sites for the generation of electricity. The two properties of water necessary for power production—head and flow—are abundant. Streamflows are

(to page 57)

Above: South of the High Lake Plateau area, looking southeast.
Top right: Aerial view of Island Lake.
Right: Viewing Mystic and Island lakes from Froze-to-Death Trail.

BEARTOOTH ALBUM

Above: The serenity of Mystic Lake.
Right: Snowbank Glacier and Summit Lake at Castle Rock Mountain.
Far right: East Rosebud River near Roscoe.

Facing page: Horseshoe Lake on Lake Plateau.

Above: Rough Lake as a mirror of the sunset.
Right: Aerial view of the Beartooths, mountaintop after mountaintop.
Right top: The Doublet.

Facing page, left: On the east side of Daisy Pass.
Right top: Black Canyon Lake.
Bottom: South face of Granite Peak from the Skytop Drainage.

Above: *Spring glory of alpine meadows.*
Right: *From Elephant Head, looking south into the Absarokas.*

Left: *The outlet of Pine Creek Lake flowing below Black Mountain.*
Above: *Rainbow Creek and Mount Douglas.*

JOHN REDDY

RICK GRAETZ

GEORGE WUERTHNER

Above: Upper Arrow Lake, Mount Villard and the Sawtooth Spires.
Top: Boulder River south of Big Timber and below the Beartooths.
Right: Jewel Lake below Black Mountain.

large and, after the spring peaks, tend to be sustained through the summer by the melting of snow and ice from the high plateaus and cirques. In addition, stream gradients are great—water falls steeply through short distances.

Enthusiasm for Beartooth hydroelectric sites is dampened by economics. Poor access and the harsh climate produce high construction and operating costs.

The Montana Power Company made a systematic search in the early part of the 20th century for a project that would serve a growing electricity demand in the Yellowstone Valley. The fruit of this search was Mystic Lake, set atop the crest of a steep head-wall on West Rosebud Creek, with a tumbling waterfall at its outlet. If the level of the lake could be raised and its water drawn from the bottom, the head and storage would be sufficient to justify the high costs. In 1916, the company filed an appropriation to use all the creek's water; by 1920, a power permit was issued by the U.S. Department of Agriculture. Construction of the facility began that year.

Tunneling to the bottom of a mountain lake underlain by hard, crystalline rock had never been successfully done, although Italian engineers had such a project under construction, to be completed in 1923. The feat was duplicated by engineers of the Montana Power Company and the DuPont Powder Company. They blew the bottom out of Mystic Lake.

Before the climactic blast, much preparation was needed. Fourteen miles of highway were built through the wilderness to the site of the power plant. More than 9,000 feet of 56-inch wood-stave pipe and a rail tram were constructed along the canyon wall from a point 1,100 feet above the power plant to the lake. A penstock 2,700 feet long was hung from the wall of the canyon.

The tunnel itself took two years to build. Its bore, seven feet in diameter and 1,000 feet long, was dug to within a few feet of the lake bottom, 50 feet below the lake's surface. In a large chamber at the end of the tunnel, a charge of 5,500 pounds of special gelatin explosive, equivalent to 10,000 pounds of dynamite, was placed. After the detonation systems were installed and the tunnel filled with water to serve as a cushion, the scene was set for the project's coup de grace.

A 1941 Montana Power Company publication describes the blast of September 25, 1924:

"At the touch of a button, the onlookers, perched high on the side of the lake, saw a great column of water rise several hundred feet in the air with a cup-shaped top. From this volleyed and thundered hundreds of tons of dirt and rock, some landing a quarter of a mile away. The earth shook with the force of the explosion and the whole canyon reverberated as if attacked by Heaven's heavy artillery. Spectators gasped and ducked for cover.

"As the waters sank, there appeared a pit-like depression. Then the whole body of the lake threw a spasm. Waves eight feet high rushed upon the beaches like tidal waves, and the surface was agitated for long minutes."

Following the completion of the generation station, a concrete arch dam was built at the outlet of the lake. The dam, 300 feet long and 45 feet high, provides 20,300 acre-feet of storage. Two 11,500 kilowatt generating units, placed in service in 1925, continue to operate today.

Reached by a three-mile hike from the parking lot at the power plant, Mystic Lake is a major recreation resource for residents of the Yellowstone Valley. Fishing is good, thanks to Lyle Piatte, the power plant manager who planted 18,000 trout eggs in the lake in 1946. The lake is the jumping-off point for climbing and hiking

trips into the wilderness, including the most popular approach to Montana's apex, Granite Peak.

The Mystic Lake project is a paradox today. When it was built, it was a remarkable engineering achievement that served the needs of a burgeoning society. Proposed today, however, the project would be controversial to a society that places high value on wilderness and the beauty of unspoiled waterfalls. It probably couldn't be built.

BEARTOOTH HIGHWAY

When Charles Kuralt, then CBS television's traveling observer of Americana, was asked to name the most beautiful road in the United States, he answered without hesitation—the Beartooth Highway. Residents of south-central Montana, not a little biased, share that view. So do countless thousands who experience this breathtaking drive each year.

The Beartooth Highway, sometimes referred to as the Red Lodge-Cooke City Highway, or simply U.S. 212, is many things to many people. To tourists it is a scenic wonder, ascending the glacier-carved walls of Rock Creek Canyon and traversing the 11,000-foot Beartooth Plateau within view of the highest peaks of a mountainous state. To engineers it is a marvel, switching back several times as it climbs the canyon cliffs. To local boosters it is a tribute to the dedicated and successful political efforts of a few visionaries who dreamed of a northeast entrance to Yellowstone National Park and a tourist industry for the depressed coal mining town of Red Lodge. To environmental purists it is an insult, intruding inappropriately into the sensitive alpine tundra, bringing thousands of automobiles and dazed tourists to a place where people should go under their own power to fully appreciate. To histori-

This page: Springtime views at the "top of the world," along the Beartooth Highway.

Facing page, top: Sunrise on the Beartooth Plateau.
Bottom: Moonset over the Beartooths.

ans, it is a fascinating story of the unlikely coincidence of political factors.

The origins of the Beartooth Highway are unknown. Native Americans undoubtedly crossed the Beartooth Plateau, even though its height tended to serve as a barrier to transportation. However, the "stockade" on the southern side of the plateau provides evidence of at least occasional visitation to the high country in the last century.

The usual route east from the Soda Butte-Clarks Fork divide region (present-day Cooke City) was the Clarks Fork River. Bannocks and other natives, and later prospectors, miners, and merchants, used this route. Where the Clarks Fork is constricted by an impassable canyon, the trail climbed steeply over Dead Indian Hill on the south side of the river.

As early as the late 1870s, however, various groups, including hunters, miners, and soldiers, sought a shorter route to the plains northeast of the Beartooth Mountains.

In 1878, after the capture of the Bannocks at the mouth of Bennett Creek on the Clarks Fork, Captain W.P. Clark of the Second Cavalry made an unsuccessful attempt to cross the plateau to Crow Agency, then located on the Stillwater River. Indians had been credited with intimate knowledge of the country, but when Clark sought to find a Crow who had been across the range or who had even head of anyone who had, he failed. To the contrary, the Crows he spoke to said it was impossible to get a horse across the mountains.

In 1880, a boundary survey attempted to follow the Montana-Wyoming state line across the plateau. Deep canyons thwarted the effort.

The first organized trip across the Beartooth Plateau was led by Lt. Gen. Phillip H. Sheridan, commander of the military division of the Missouri. The U.S. army was active in the affairs of Yellowstone National Park. The road from

Bozeman to Fort Yellowstone was well established. But in 1877 the Yellowstone Valley had been "liberated" from the natives and a route to the national park from the east was desired, as was a shorter route from the park to Crow Agency.

In 1881, Sheridan, with 124 men, 83 horses, and 183 mules, visited Yellowstone National Park from the east. After exploring the Bighorn Mountains, the expedition passed Pryor's Gap and camped near Bridger's road where it crossed the Clarks Fork River. At the mouth of the Clarks Fork canyon, Sheridan was awed. He compared the 24-mile-long, 3,000-foot-deep gorge with the canyons of the Yellowstone, the Arkansas, the Animas, and the Colorado.

Crossing over Dead Indian Hill, the contingent reached the edge of the Beartooth Plateau and viewed Pilot Knob and Index Peak, which he called "…The great landmarks of the Rocky Mountains." Sheridan, intrigued by the plateau, decided to return to pioneer a route across it to the plains. The next year he did.

In 1882, Sheridan led another expedition to Yellowstone, this time by way of Ft. Washakie and Fort Ellis, near Bozeman, entering the park through the canyons of the Yellowstone River. Leaving the park via Cooke City, the party met a Park City hunter named Geer who claimed to have a route across the plateau to the plains. Against the advice of his older guides, Sheridan engaged Geer to lead the way.

Geer led them across the Clarks Fork, then northeast up the slopes of the plateau. Wild game was abundant and Sheridan was impressed with the beauty of the alpine wildflowers and the spectacular panoramas. Geer's route to the plains descended Littlerock Creek to the Clarks Fork. Although the trail was unmarked and steep, there was only one minor mishap (a mule fell from the trail and landed in the top of a tree) and no casualties. In retrospect, Sheridan wished he had gone straight east and descended Line Creek to a point closer to Bridger's crossing of the Clarks Fork. Nevertheless, he had proved a point. The plateau could be crossed by horses. It was left to hunters and miners to find the most feasible route.

A trail was pioneered up the east side of Mount Maurice, south of Red Lodge, to the Line Creek Plateau. This so-called "Black and White Trail" shortened the traverse to Cooke City considerably. But a more efficient route still was needed.

Ed Van Dyke is credited with that accomplishment. Well before the turn of the 20th century, this eccentric hunter had established his "Slickrock Trail" from his outpost at Wolf Creek on the upper Clarks Fork, over the plateau, and down the talus into Rock Creek. From there it was an easy ride to Red Lodge. For years, Van Dyke made an annual trek to Red Lodge with twenty to thirty pack ponies laden with elk and bear meat.

Folks were not satisfied with the steep and difficult Slickrock and Black and White trails. Cooke City miners and mineral speculators had waged a long, frustrating, and unsuccessful battle for improved access to the New World Mining District. The administrators of Yellowstone National Park, both civilian and military, desired a northeast entrance to the park. And Red Lodge business interests wanted to diversify the local economy by adding tourism. A natural answer was the Beartooth Highway.

As early as 1919, Dr. J.C.F. Siegfriedt, a Bear Creek physician, solicited federal aid for a road to follow the Black and White Trail. The route was later abandoned in favor of the current one, but Siegfriedt and O.H.P. Shelley, the local newspaper editor, succeeded in enlisting an essential ally. Congressman Scott Leavitt, elected in 1922, became their champion.

Leavitt, a Republican and a former forester, agreed to sponsor the Park Approach Act. As originally proposed, this legislation would have authorized a major national program of access roads to national parks. In the modest form in which it passed in 1931, only one proposal survived—the Beartooth Highway.

In the meantime, it wasn't easy convincing Congress that an expensive road over an 11,000-foot plateau was in the public interest. In 1925, the U.S. Forest Service and the Bureau of Public Roads had conducted a joint study on the feasibility of the project. Despite heavy coercion, the report's authors concluded that the road would not be feasible for mining purposes.

About the same time, Dr. Siegfriedt led a delegation to Washington to try to convince Secretary of the Interior Albert Fall of the merits of the idea. Fall, later convicted of illegal activity in the Teapot Dome scandal, called for a report from the U.S. Bureau of Mines on the viability of the New World Mining District at Cooke City. The report was unfavorable and Fall dismissed the delegation.

Encouraged by the Montana congressional delegation and despite the unfavorable feasibility report, the Bureau of Public Roads continued to study the proposed project. In 1927, a survey party led by Harry Mitchell conducted a field reconnaissance. As a result of investigations of several routes over the plateau, the party began to favor a tunnel. Significant costs could be saved in construction and maintenance by a tunnel avoiding the heights of the plateau.

But the party received a surprise visit from Congressman Leavitt who rode on horseback with the engineers and viewed the various alternatives. He warmly endorsed the higher, more scenic route and assured the engineers that Senators Walsh and Wheeler shared his views on the subject. He was convinced that the recreational benefits of an alpine highway would justify the costs.

Siegfriedt and his associates were encouraged—with good reason. Firmly behind the congressional bill were not only Congressman Leavitt, but also two of the most powerful men in the U.S. Senate—Thomas Walsh and Burton Wheeler, members of the so-called Silver block. By January of 1931, the Montana congressional delegation had secured passage of the legislation.

Preparation of the route began that year, and, in 1932, construction was under way. By 1936, the road was oiled and officially opened to tourist travel. Congress obediently continued to provide the appropriations necessary to complete the job, despite dramatic changes in the Montana Congressional delegation.

Scott Leavitt, five-term representative, was defeated in 1932, a bad year for Republicans. In addition to the national Roosevelt landslide, Leavitt's constituents became increasingly intolerant of his staunch support for prohibition. He ran for the U.S. Senate in 1934, won the primary, but lost the general election badly. He retired from politics and returned to the Forest Service.

Senator Tom Walsh, in his early 70s, enjoyed immense prestige in the Senate and was tapped by President Roosevelt to be attorney general. But Walsh, returning from a Havana vacation with his Cuban bride of a few days, died in North Carolina.

So, the Montana congressional delegation was seriously weakened. Had the Park Approach Act not passed in 1931 or 1932, it probably never would have. The Beartooth Plateau would have been saved from the insult of a tourist highway. And literally millions of motorists, including Charles Kuralt, wouldn't have experienced the thrill of America's most beautiful highway.

HAROLD UREY

The Beartooth Mountains consist of some of the oldest rocks ever found on the planet. These rocks have played important roles in the development of theories about the origin and age of the earth and its solar system. One of the central figures in the development was Harold Urey, Nobel Prize winner and Montana's most eminent scientist.

Urey was born in 1893 in Indiana. After graduating from high school and teaching at a country school, he moved to Montana to be near his family, who had settled on a ranch near Big Timber. Harold got a job teaching at the Glasston school, near the foot of the Beartooth Mountains. Staring at the massive uplift of the mountains and the snow-clad crystalline heights of the plateaus stirred his wonder about the rocks, their makeup, and their origin.

After a year, Urey transferred to the Chimney Rock school, on the Trail Creek divide, south of Livingston. From there, he could again marvel at the giant uplift of the mountains and see the ancient rocks at their summits. He knew he could never be content with a career teaching at country schools.

Influenced by his friend Bryan Wilson of Big Timber, Urey enrolled at Montana State University (now the University of Montana) at Missoula in the fall of 1914, intending to major in psychology. He graduated in 1917 with a major in zoology and a minor in chemistry. After a stint as a research chemist with a chemical company in Baltimore, Urey returned to the university in Missoula to teach. In 1921 he began a doctoral program in physical chemistry at the University of California, completing the degree in 1923. A year's study under Niels Bohr in Copenhagen stimulated his fertile mind about the makeup of molecules and atoms.

At Columbia University Urey continued his research into the depths of the atom and in 1934 he was awarded the Nobel Prize in chemistry for his discovery of heavy water. He had unlocked the door to the atomic age.

In his later life Harold Urey had misgivings about the technological directions taken by our society. He turned his career to other fields of inquiry: geology, astrochemistry, geochemistry, and cosmology. He pondered the origin of the earth and the solar system. And he pondered the rocks he had contemplated as a young educator in the shadow of the Beartooth Mountains.

Urey died in 1981. In 1990, the University of Montana named the Harold C. Urey Lecture Hall in his honor.

THE EARLY CLIMBERS

FRED INABNIT

On April 29,1929, the National Geographic Board designated the mountain south of East Rosebud Lake as Mount Inabnit, in honor of Fred Inabnit, long-time Beartooth mountaineer. Inabnit, a Swiss, harbored a love for the mountains and the alpine that led him from his home in Billings to the trailless Beartooth at every opportunity. Fred's favorite mountain—Granite Peak—already had a name, but the first peak he climbed in the Beartooth made a fitting namesake.

Inabnit was three years old when his father, a cabinetmaker, brought his family to the United States. Reared in Indiana and Wisconsin, he taught school and developed a good working knowledge of geology and the natural sciences. After moving to Montana in 1890, he worked in a store in the long-since-vanished town of Ubet in the Judith Basin. In 1893 he moved to Billings and was employed by the Yegen store and later as a cashier in the Yegen Bank. At the age of forty, he discovered the Beartooth Mountains.

RICK GRAETZ

At the turn of the 20th century, the remote height of the range had rarely been visited. Indeed, it was no mean feat to so much as approach the mountains in the days before automobiles and roads.

Inabnit's first expedition to the Beartooth was in 1907. With three companions, he traveled in a lumber wagon over a boulder-strewn road to Armstrong Lake, now East Rosebud Lake. While at the lake, the adventurers used a cabin built in the late 1800s by Indian Agent H.J. Armstrong, then owned by Christian Yegen of Billings and John Chapman of Red Lodge.

After a two-day rest at the lake, the quartet, laden with sixty-pound packs, tested the mountains—and themselves. Climbing "the Snowbanks," now Mount Inabnit, they passed the silver spray of Snow Falls and reached the summit of the ridge above the glacier. Greeting them, Inabnit later wrote, was "a magnificent expanse of rugged wastes, dotted with blue, gem-like lakes and glittering glaciers, falling from the granite shoulders of massive peaks... a land of grim splendor." They hiked the plateau, peering into 2,000-foot chasms, skirting unnamed lakes, resting in aster-filled meadows, and drinking from icy streams. Across the head of the East Rosebud, they scanned the forest wilderness of the Clarks Fork, then turned to view the challenge that lured Inabnit for the rest of his life—the lofty comb-like crest of Granite Peak.

Above: *From above Wounded Man Lake.*
Left: *Looking across the Boulder River toward the Crow Mountains.*

Facing page: *South face of Granite Peak.*

The group returned footsore, sunburned, wind-battered, and weary. But the experience was gripping—Inabnit was to spend the rest of his life with the Beartooth.

Summer after summer, Inabnit crisscrossed the range. He ascended East and West Rosebud creeks, the Stillwater River, the forks of Rock Creek, and the Boulder River. He roamed the plateaus—Silver Run, Hellroaring, Line Creek, Red Lodge Creek, East Rosebud, Lake, and Fish-tail. He camped by the placid lakes—Goose, Avalanche, Elk, Rainbow, Rimrock, Deep, Snow, Mystic, Timberline, Beartooth, Long, Rock Island, Wounded Man, and countless unnamed tarns. He glissaded the snowfields and glaciers—Skytop, Grasshopper, Snowbank, Sundance, Hidden, and Wolf. He visited the tourist traps—Cooke City's Curl Hotel, the Dickinson Ranch (later, Nordquist's L Bar T), Johnson's Sawtooth Ranch, Hickock's Beartooth Lodge, Richel Lodge, Camp Senia, Shaw's Camp at Goose Lake, and Beartooth Ranch. All the while, he flirted with Granite Peak.

As early as 1910, Inabnit seriously approached Granite with the thought of scaling its serrated summit. From Mount Tempest, he scanned the east ridge with binoculars and concluded that a better route must be found. Crossing Granite Creek and the pass to Skytop Creek, his party was turned back by an intense August snowstorm.

In 1922, Inabnit led a well-equipped and well-coordinated party of five enthusiastic climbers to the peak, approaching from the south by way of Skytop Creek. The group scaled to within 300 feet of the summit before being halted by sheer walls.

In 1923, the undaunted Inabnit persuaded the already-interested U.S. Forest Service to participate in a joint venture. From a camp near Avalanche Lake, the party split into two assault teams. Inabnit led his group into Skytop Creek for another attempt at the south face. The Forest Service group, led by Elers Koch, scaled the east ridge. As Inabnit and his party were again blocked by vertical cliffs, they heard the triumphant shouts of the rangers above. Although not a member of the summit team, Inabnit, at age fifty-seven, took enormous pride in his role in the first ascent of Montana's highest peak.

In 1926, at Shaw's Goose Lake Camp, Inabnit fell in with Norman Clyde, a Sierra Clubber and well-known mountaineer. Clyde, who had recently climbed the Grand Teton, was intrigued with Granite Peak; Inabnit offered the services of his party as guides. Clyde made the second successful ascent of Granite, accompanied by Ernest Vogel, one of Inabnit's companions. On his return, Vogel allowed that he never could have reached the summit without the assistance of the experienced Clyde. From that moment on, Inabnit realized that Granite Peak would never be his.

Fred Inabnit died in November of 1928, only a few days after election to a fourth term as Clerk of the Court in Billings. He had served his community as school board member, city alderman, and county treasurer. But he is remembered most for his undying devotion to the Beartooth, which he experienced in a way and at a time no one else did.

Peter Koch

Growing up in Denmark, young Peter Koch could hardly comprehend the grand scale of American geography. A thirst to experience such expansiveness, coupled with rejection by the woman he loved, provided all the impetus needed for the young divinity student to leave the university and see America.

Arriving in the United States in the late 1860s, Peter knocked around the east for a couple of years, then visited an uncle in Mississippi. Koch saw little opportunity in the south, so he set out to explore the great American west. After a stint as a wood cutter on the Musselshell he wrote in his diary: "Twenty-five years old today, and still poor as a church rat." Moving on, he settled in the Gallatin Valley where Nelson Story, the prominent rancher and merchant, gave him a job. Koch eventually prospered, becoming cashier and vice president of the Bozeman National Bank and a prominent citizen of the community.

While Peter Koch was learning the skills of a frontiersman, he was also a serious student of the environment. He observed vegetation, wildlife, and geology. He made maps and entered daily weather data in his diary. As his profession al-

lowed, he concentrated more and more on enjoying and studying the Montana outdoors, all the while infecting his sons, Elers and Stanley, with his love of nature.

Indeed Peter Koch came to be respected as an expert amateur botanist. As he traveled the state, he collected plants and contributed to the early understanding of the botany of Montana. Much of his plant collecting was done in the Gallatin and Madison ranges south of Bozeman; on one trip, the trio of Koch and his sons climbed what later was to be named Koch Peak, a prominent crag of the Madison Range and the centerpiece of the Taylor Peaks.

One of Koch's favorite areas was the Beartooth. In the summers of 1897 and 1899, he made treks to Yellowstone National Park by way of the high plateaus of the Boulder and the Stillwater, collecting plants en route. He took specimens from the Granite Range, from the Lake Plateau, and on the Clarks Fork River. Many of these specimens are in the collection of the Montana State University Herbarium.

One of Koch's most extensive trips took place in the summer of 1897. With Elers and Stanley, aged fifteen and sixteen, along with Professors Reid, Traphagen, and Wilcox of the college faculty, Dr. Moore, a Presbyterian minister from Helena, and a packer and cook, Peter set out from Bozeman on horseback to explore the Beartooth Mountains and Yellowstone National Park. The party traveled over Bozeman Pass to Livingston, then up the Boulder River, and over Boulder Pass to Cooke City, which stood almost abandoned at the time. The riders entered Yellowstone Park through a back door—down the Clarks Fork, up Crandall Creek, over Hoodoo Basin, and into the Lamar Valley.

Unbeknownst to Koch and his party, the Park

had recently been the scene of a series of stage-coach robberies. As the unsuspecting Bozeman tourists approached the Grand Canyon, three weeks in the saddle and looking not unlike a gang of renegades, they were detained by the army, responsible at the time for policing the park. Elers Koch remembered the scene this way.

"A hardboiled old time sergeant of the regular army was in charge of the Canyon post. We were brought into his quarters for an examination. My father appeared first as spokesman for the party. He identified himself as Peter Koch, vice president and director of the Bozeman National Bank, an elder in the Presbyterian Church, and a generally well known and reputable citizen. Next up was Dr. James Reid, tall and dignified, but with one shirt sleeve half torn off, fuming with the indignity of such treatment. He was President of the State College, an ordained minister, and a man accustomed to more respect. Then came Dr. Moore, who was minister of the Presbyterian Church in Helena. Then Mr. Wilcox. He was a great big burly man, dressed very carelessly with a black stubble of beard, and no stage robber could have better looked the part, but he claimed to be a doctor of philosophy and head of the biology department of the college at Bozeman. The sergeant looked at him incredulously and called the next man, Dr. Traphagen, who was head of the department of geology and chemistry at the college. The doctor was a very gentle kindly appearing man with big brown eyes and a pointed Vandyke beard. Before he could open his mouth the old sergeant decided he had had enough. 'I suppose you are going to tell me you are Jesus Christ,' he bellowed. Two days passed before the identities of the group could be established to the satisfaction of the disconcerted authorities."

The decision of Peter's son Elers to become a forester was no surprise, given the interest and companionship of his father. While on summer break from his course of general studies at the state college at Bozeman, Elers got a job with the U.S. Bureau of Forestry. Soon thereafter, Gifford Pinchot, the head of the bureau, visited the Tacoma camp and made a lasting impression on the young Koch.

In the year before Koch graduated in 1901, the Yale School of Forestry had been established under the auspices of Pinchot. Koch enrolled and, two years later, was one of the first professionally trained foresters in the country. After graduation in 1903 he went to work for the Bureau of Forestry as one of Pinchot's "young men." Along with others he worked out of Washington, D.C., writing reports and drawing maps in the winter and making field inspections and boundary surveys in the summer. The fruits of the labors of Koch and his colleagues, under the guidance of Gifford Pinchot, was the national forest system.

In December of 1906, at the age of twenty-six, Koch returned to Montana to be the supervisor of the Lolo, Bitterroot, and Missoula national forests. In that same year, he married Gerda Heigerg-Jurgensen from Denmark, daughter of the woman who had rejected his father in the 1860s.

Elers Koch served as forest supervisor for eleven years, then advanced to the position of district (regional) fire chief. After two years in that post, he became assistant district forester and chief of the Division of Timber Management, where he served until his retirement in 1944.

Of his many achievements, Koch placed special value on one: on August 27, 1923, he led the first successful climb to the summit of Granite Peak, the highest point in Montana and the crown of the Beartooth.

James P. Kimball

James P. Kimball, geologist and mining engineer, led a pioneering expedition to the high peaks of the Beartooth in 1898. Funded by the Rockefeller family and the Rocky Fork Coal Company, Kimball searched for minerals and attempted to map the region between Cooke City and Nye. Bad weather disrupted his mapping and the crystalline rocks revealed no precious metals, but today's maps are decorated with names left by the group.

Born in 1836, Kimball was educated at Harvard and at the University of Gottingen in Germany, where he took his A.M. and Ph.D. degrees. He served the state geological surveys of Wisconsin and Illinois, taught chemistry and economic geology at the New York State Agricultural College, then served in the Civil War under Gens. Patrick, McClellan, Burnside, Hooker, and Meade. In 1885, after a stint at Leigh University, he was named director of the U.S. Mint in Washington, D.C.

In 1898 Kimball recruited seven men to accompany him to the highest peaks in the Beartooth, known then as the Granite Range. His photographer was Anders Wilse, a young Norwegian living in Seattle; others in the party included A.B. Wood and Russell Kimball.

Kimball, regarding the massive Beartooth uplift as unvisited and unmapped, called it a "terra incognita and a mystery for nearly a quarter century past." The only signs of human occupation he found were a few aboriginal arrowheads and obsidian chips picked up near the crest of the range. "The inevitable and irrepressible tin can, which mainly constitutes the kitchen midden of the present nomad the world over, was conspicuous by its absence."

Outfitted in Bozeman with eight saddle and nine pack animals, the party reached Cooke City on July 24, 1898. There, Kimball observed: "A summer climate at high altitudes finer than that of Cooke would be difficult to find and a more attractive landscape hardly possible." His joy with Eden was dampened, however, by horseflies: "From these vampires there is no escape."

The mission of the expedition was to complete a plane-table survey which would join the published sheets of the U.S.G.S. to the north. Beginning at Cooke City, the party hacked a trail up Crazy and Russell creeks to the East Rosebud divide. From a camp at Fossil Lake (they called it Island Lake), and after inclement weather had quashed initial attempts, the trekkers climbed Mt. Dewey and named it "in honor of a friend, the echo of whose valiant exploits at Manila reached the surveying party at Cooke."

From Pavement Pass, Wood, Wilse, and Russell Kimball made a trail to a bivouac at Goose Lake. They explored Grasshopper Glacier, named for the grasshopper remains that constituted the morainal material fringing the lower edge of the glacier. From this unique mass of ice, no fragment could be broken so small that it did not contain grasshopper remains. The surveyors were duly enthralled by this natural wonder.

Traversing the range to the north of Goose Lake, Wilse and Wood climbed and named Mt. Villard (for Henry Villard, a builder of the Northern Pacific Railroad), Mt. Spofford (now Glacier Peak, for C.A. Spofford), Mt. Fox (for Dr. J.M. Fox of Red Lodge), Mt. Wilse, Mt. Wood, and Mt. Hague (for geologist Arnold Hague). They attempted to climb Granite Peak, but were thwarted at an elevation of 11,447 (estimated by their aneroid barometer), well below the 12,799-foot summit. Because of the ruggedness of the

terrain, they carried neither Wilse's photographic equipment nor the plane table.

After five days in the craggiest country in Montana, the pair rendezvoused with the other members of the party, which had descended the Stillwater River on horseback.

Kimball, then in his sixties, published a map and an article describing his adventure. Soon thereafter he retired to Cody, Wyoming, not far from his last great field trip. He died in Cody in 1913.

Above: Poma lifts are the signs of a ski camp at Twin Lakes.
Right: Atop Granite Peak.
Top right: Cedar Lake.

Facing page, top: Skytop Creek.
Bottom: Lake Abundance and the Slough Creek corridor.

The Photographer

Anders Wilse was a young Norwegian photographer who decided to give America a try in the 1890s. After knocking around the midwest for a couple of years, he settled in Seattle, a community populous with Scandinavians, and established a business selling photos and maps. After about a year, he had began to make a name for himself and was invited by James Kimball to accompany a Rockefeller-sponsored expedition to the wilds of Montana. The wages were good and he would be able to retain all of the photos he took.

Wilse's job as photographer was to prepare a map of the Granite Range with the aid of photographs, a plane table a barometer, and a compass. In addition, the entire party was to look for minerals. Perhaps the most enduring legacy of Kimball's Beartooth expedition is the work of Anders Wilse, several of whose prints were reproduced in Kimball's article in an 1899 *Bulletin of the American Geographic Society of New York*. The Montana Historical Society Library holds several Wilse prints, but the approximately 160 plates taken by Wilse in the Beartooth and assembled by the artist in a portfolio were presumably taken to Norway when he returned there a few years later. Of Wilse, Kimball wrote: "The views taken were at the cost of indefatigable labor and hardy endurance on the part of the photographer who combines with professional skill in the field of photography rare accomplishments as a topographer, along with sturdy qualities as a mountaineer."

Wilse's photographs of the country around Granite Peak, north of Cooke City, are stunning. Wilse later published a book that chronicled his adventures. Written in Norwegian, the book is excerpted and loosely translated here.

"We were told by hunters in slightly mystical undertones that far up in the mountains there was a mountain with a glacier full of grasshoppers. We didn't attach much value to this story, but one day I climbed up to the top of a 12,000-foot mountain in order to take measurements of the direction of a watercourse. I had completed my observations when I looked down at the foot of the mountain. Here I saw a remarkable sight. It was a glacier—but one with a surface which looked like the skin of an elephant. I went down to it and found that the stripes that went sideways across it were piles of dead grasshoppers. At the foot of the glacier there were railroad car-sized loads of shells, bodies, and legs of grasshoppers. In the crevasses of the glacier I could see thick layers of these insects. Far down in the crevasse I could see one layer of grasshoppers and one of ice, and then grasshoppers again. I filled my flask with samples and I tell you there was a stir in camp when I came back and described my discovery! The mountain on which I discovered this I named Mt. Wilse.

"From this glacier flowed a rather large river which we could not place properly on the map. We couldn't even figure out where it went when it reached the mapped areas to the north. So another engineer (A.B. Wood) and I got the task of charting the river. Outfitted with a wool blanket apiece, ten days of provisions on our backs and with good solid boots and clothes, we took off.

"The fifth day we reached the top of a mountain to take observations. To our great happiness, we saw that under us stretched the prairie on the other side of the mountains from which we had started and behind us lay a wild mountain landscape with glittering glaciers.

"So it was. But to descend to the foothills was no easy task. Finally we found a little valley where, with the help of bushes for handholds, we came down to the bottom, which was covered with high yellowed grass. When we got down, we scared up a tremendous cloud of grasshoppers and as we went further, the cloud steadily grew. Now, besides answering the mystery of where the glacial river came down to the prairie we had answered the mystery of grasshoppers on the glacier.

"During the fall, grasshopper swarms gather in this river valley in order to emigrate over the mountain range. Following the river to the high country, they perhaps met a snowstorm, fell, and became buried. In spring the snow became ice and put down a new layer on the glacier. Where there are layers on the glacier in which there are no grasshoppers, either the grasshoppers did not emigrate that year or they came over the pass successfully."

Upon reaching the prairie, the Kimball expedition received a letter which had to be answered

Anders Wilse's panoramas of Grasshopper Glacier on the mountain he named for himself.

immediately. Wilse was given the task of delivering the response. He took off with Pussy, his pony, on a forty-mile crosscountry trip, following the Stillwater River toward Cooke City. At the pass he and Pussy found themselves with steep cliffs on all the possible descents. Somehow he got his horse through the rugged talus and rockslides, reaching town in time for the post. The rest of the expedition came back two days later. The guides could not believe he had come the way he did and survived.

"One of the scouts said, 'What the hell is a guy with only two months of mountain experience doing here?' It was like a kick in the ass to me—a comment for which I long wanted to make him eat his words. The chance finally came when he had gone out hunting and we met each other on the way back to camp. I had my big photography apparatus on my back and a heavy tripod in my hands. He offered to carry the tripod for me, for which I was grateful, because I was really worn out.

"Then we came to a steep mountain cliff where there was a narrow shelf, about a foot wide. Under that cliff the river was racing. Our course was such that either we used the narrow shelf or took a very long way around. I chose to go over the shelf with my face plastered against the cliff wall.

When I had reached the other side I looked back and saw that Mr. John still stood on the other side and motioned that he intended to go around. I went back across and took the tripod from him. Still he didn't dare to move. I went back, took his rifle, and talked him across the passage.

"In the camp he asked my pardon for what he had said about 'two month mountaineers'."

Mammals

The Beartooth Mountains are home to many members of the animal kingdom, among them birds, fish, insects, spiders, rotifers, and worms. The ones of primary interest to most people are the mammals.

At one extreme in the range of mammals is the dwarf shrew, tipping the analytical balance at less than a quarter of an ounce. The first Montana specimens of this tiny dynamo were collected on the Beartooth Plateau in 1958. At the other extreme are the moose, weighing in at sometimes more than a thousand pounds, and the bison, sometimes reaching a ton.

The best known of the mammals are the game animals—elk, deer, moose, bighorn sheep, mountain goats, and black bear. Others that stir the excitement are grizzly, bison, marten, coyote and (possibly) wolves.

The most common of the mammals are the rodents. Marmots, squirrels, chipmunks, and ground squirrels may be seen on almost any summer day in any part of the range. In the talus slopes of higher elevation, but also occasionally in lower elevations, the pika, or cony, greets visitors with its distinctive nasal "meow."

The diminutive pikas act like they own the Beartooth. They are generally wary of people and oth-

ANIMALS OF THE ALPINE WORLD

ERWIN & PEGGY BAUER

er predators, diving into the rocks at the first threat. Sometimes, though, they can be in a hay gathering frenzy and be oblivious to climbers and hikers. Their hay piles are emergency winter supplies, tapped when snow cover is poor, ruling out subniveal grazing.

Nearly forty species of mammals have been observed in the alpine of the Beartooth. Most of these are summer visitors. The porcupine and the red squirrel, for example, traverse the alpine in migration. Bears and badgers sporadically exploit the resources of the alpine.

These mammals are year-round residents of the alpine Beartooth: montane dwarf and northern water shrews; heather, montane and water voles; short-tailed and long-tailed weasels; pikas; white-tailed jackrabbits; yellow-bellied marmots; northern pocket gophers; deer mice; bighorn sheep; and mountain goats. In addition, golden-mantled ground squirrels and least chipmunks probably hibernate in the alpine. And—documented in the 1990s—the red fox survives in the winter on the plateau.

The mountain fox is a puzzler because the red fox is usually associated with the lowlands. In the high country of the Beartooth and Yellowstone National Park, it is often gray and sometimes a

Above: Pine marten.
Top: Red fox.
Left: Bull moose.

Facing page: Mountain goat.

creamy, bleached red. Its presence raises some perplexing questions. Is this mountain fox a unique subspecies? If so, which one? Is it a pure remnant of a refugial population from the Wisconsin glaciation? Did it migrate down an ice-free corridor in the last continental ice sheet? Did lowland foxes disperse into the Beartooth? Perhaps DNA fingerprinting will provide some answers.

At the back of this book is a list of the mammals that have been observed on the alpine Beartooth Plateau.

ELK

The Yellowstone elk herds, both northern and southern, are famous, partly because of the controversies related to their management.

In 1872, Congress had yet to hear about the ecosystem concept in natural resource management. It had, however, heard of the wonders of the upper Yellowstone—the fabulous thermal features, the abundant wildlife, the spectacular canyons and rivers. It set aside Yellowstone National Park.

That legislation was unprecedented. No other country had shown enough foresight to preserve a national park. But as farsighted as the decision was, it was flawed—the rectangular boundary of the park took no account of the natural boundaries of watersheds or animal migration routes. The result was difficult management of the park's resources. At the head of the list of management controversies has been the "elk problem."

Evidence, theory, and opinion are divided on the question of the abundance of wildlife in the Yellowstone Park area prior to the 1870s. After 1878, however, most visitors spoke of the great numbers of elk and other animals. In 1899, the northern Yellowstone herd was estimated at 60,000 head.

Elk spend their summers in the high country of the Yellowstone's tributaries, some inside the park, and some along the south-flowing streams that drain the volcanic peaks of the western Beartooth. As winter snowfall drives the animals downslope, they migrate to their winter range in the Yellowstone Valley, downstream from the park boundary.

Hunting is not allowed in the park. Yet the elk's natural predators such as the wolf have been virtually eliminated. The result is a herd that many biologists consider too large for the winter range in the valley. To make matters worse, the elk often have a hard time getting to the winter range.

As the elk cross the park line, they are eligible for human predation—hunting. The "firing line" near Jardine has been infamous for its carnage and also for driving the elk back into the park.

The problem was recognized not long after the turn of the 20th century. During the 1870s, the Yellowstone Valley was stocked with cattle. By 1914 it was clear that the valley was overgrazed. By 1926 the condition of the range was so bad it was thought that artificial seeding would be needed for recovery.

In 1911, hunters made the first heavy slaughter near Gardiner. The Forest Service and the Biological Survey (now the U.S. Fish and Wildlife Service) began to study the problem. The report, issued in 1917, recommended withdrawing land in the elks' winter range from entry under the public land laws. It was done.

In 1926, the winter range was added to the Gallatin and Absaroka national forests and provisions were made for acquiring private lands for additional winter range. At the same time, cattle grazing was curtailed. The effect was positive and condition of the range improved. But it wasn't enough.

The problem and its controversy continue today. The park boundary continues to immobilize the game managers of Montana. With the development of the oriental market for antler-based tonics, poaching—an age-old problem in Yellowstone—has increased. Winter range condition has improved, but home-building in the valley near Gardiner has cut into the effective size of the range.

But some progress has been made. Since 1988, the Rocky Mountain Elk Foundation, working cooperatively with the U.S. Forest Service, the National Park Service, and the Montana Department of Fish, Wildlife and Parks, has closed a dozen land acquisition deals between Dome Mountain and the Park boundary. By 1994 nearly 9,000 acres of private winter range had been added to the public domain at a cost of about $10 million.

The Beartooth Mountains provide winter and summer range for elk other than those of the northern Yellowstone herd. A resident herd uses the western flank of the range along the Yellowstone Valley from Cedar Creek north to about Strawberry Creek.

The north front of the range, as far east as Line Creek, is winter range for five elk herds that summer in the Beartooth high country.

• The East Boulder Plateau herd winters in both the Main Boulder and the Stillwater valleys. The herd has about 400 head in the Main Boulder, 250 on the West Boulder, 100 to 150 on the East Boulder River and Deer creeks, and about 150 on the Stillwater.

• The West Rosebud herd, about 250 head, winters mostly on the MacKay Ranch between the East and West Rosebuds.

• The Butcher Creek herd winters east of the East Rosebud. It numbers about 75.

• The Silver Run herd of about 250 head winters on Rock Creek.

• The Line Creek herd summers in both Wyoming and Montana but winters mostly in Montana in the Line Creek/Ruby Creek area. It numbers between 300 and 400.

The herds in the West Fork of Rock Creek and the Line Creek Plateau have expanded onto the prairie in recent times.

GRIZZLY

The grizzly bear is one of Americas best symbols of free, wild, and natural wildlife. Its size is awesome—adult males may reach half a ton. Its often aggressive but usually unpredictable behavior gives it both respect and mystique.

Much of the southern half of the Absaroka-Beartooth is home to the grizzly. Although few bears live exclusively in this area, the ranges of many extend into the south-flowing tributaries of the Yellowstone River—Hellroaring Creek, Buffalo Fork, and Slough Creek—as well as the lower elevations of the Beartooth Plateau. Bears have been sighted or radio-tracked across the Beartooth from its east side to its northern edge near Livingston. Wherever elk winter, bears emerge from dens and gorge on spring carrion. In the summer, bears graze riparian forests and subalpine meadows for the succulent vegetation that comprises nearly 80 percent of their diet.

The grizzly bear is a threatened species in the lower 48 states. In the Greater Yellowstone ecosystem, which includes the Absaroka-Beartooth, the grizzly population was estimated at 236 in 1993. That's about the same number of bears in the ecosystem 20 years before. Although federal bear managers believe the production of cubs has improved, mortality has declined, and overall population trends are up, human-caused mortality and the steady loss of the bear's habitat have combined to perpetuate a tenuous situation of alarm.

It wasn't always so. When Lewis and Clark ventured into present-day Montana, they encountered grizzlies all across the prairie. But white settlement had no place for the bear, which people viewed as a threat to their lives, livestock, and livelihoods. The bear was extirpated on the prairie and nearly reduced to a remnant population in the mountains. There, the bear was hunted for its impressive trophies of hide, claws and teeth and for bragging rights to the killing of the largest North American carnivore.

In the lower forty-eight states, only six ecosystems retain grizzlies. Of these, only one, the northern continental divide of Glacier National Park and the Bob Marshall wilderness complex, is considered marginally healthy. Four—the Cabinets, the Selkirks, the Selway Bitterroots, and the north Cascades—have populations so low they must be considered remnants.

The Greater Yellowstone ecosystem has perhaps the most famous population of grizzlies. Generations of Americans think of bears when they think of Yellowstone. The grizzlies of the Park have been the focus of attention and controversy since the late 1960s and early 1970s.

After grizzlies killed two women in Glacier National Park in separate incidents on August 15, 1967, the National Park Service recognized the need to change its bear policies. The most drastic change involved closing the dumps which had served as food sources and centers of socialization for bears since before the turn of the century. The new philosophy of the Park Service was to return the bears to natural feeding instantly—"cold turkey." Predictably, human-bear encounters increased as the dismayed ursids sought food in the next best places—campgrounds. A human-bear encounter almost always led to the bear's demise. Yellowstone's population took a precipitous drop.

Controversy over the bear continues. Scientists, politicians, conservationists, bureaucrats, outfitters, and the general public disagree on how the great bear should be managed. On some important things there is general agreement, however. Most importantly, our society has agreed that the bear should survive in the lower 48 states, including the Greater Yellowstone ecosystem. In 1975, the grizzly was listed as threatened under the Endangered Species Act. Under the terms of that pioneering legislation, no federal agency may take an action that reduces the numbers, reproduction, or distribution of an endangered or threatened species and appreciably diminishes the prospects for its survival. The grizzly lives mostly on federal lands.

Two things seem clear. Mortality must be minimized so that deaths do not exceed births. And the bear's habitat must be preserved and protected. Neither of these things will be easy.

To minimize mortality, human–bear encounters must be minimized. That means ensuring that commercial and private camps are clean and do not serve as attractants for bears. Sheep must not be grazed where bears live. During the critical springs and fall months bears should have exclusive use of their range.

The bear's habitat cannot be nibbled away. Each timber sale, mine, ski area, or oil and gas well may not in itself threaten the continued survival of the bear. Taken collectively, however, those developments could spell doom for the grizzly. Therefore, the cumulative impacts of all development proposals must be considered when a decision is made on each of them.

What are the prospects for the bear? It's not clear. Most agency personnel, who now have both a commitment to the bear and a bag full of management tools, are optimistic. Others are not so

Above: Grizzly bear.
Right: Bull elk.
Bottom left: Porcupine.
Bottom right: Mule deer buck in velvet.

Left: Bighorn ram.
Above: *Mountain goats.*
Top: *Yellow-bellied marmot.*

sanguine, especially conservationists who view with alarm the steady loss of habitat and with skepticism the posture of agencies that we can have resource development and bears in the same places. Only time and the continuing commitment of vigilant citizens will tell. And therein lies the brightest ray of hope for the bear—a strong, vocal, and growing national constituency stands firmly in the bear's corner.

Bighorn Sheep

In the 1800s, bighorns were common throughout the west. Lewis and Clark sighted them all along their route. The population was estimated at 2 million in 1880.

With the introduction of domestic livestock into Montana, the bighorns fared poorly. Range competition and overuse led to malnutrition and die-offs due to scabies, anthrax, lungworm, and pneumonia.

By the 1930s, bighorns existed only in small,

isolated bands. By 1940, the sheep were considered endangered; the herds were unhealthy and unproductive. In the 1970s and 1980s, critical winter range was protected by fencing and competition from livestock was reduced. As a result, at least three herds are known by their winter ranges, on which they live about eight months of each year.

The smallest herd, which numbers about eleven, winters in the Rock Creek and Line Creek drainages south of Red Lodge. Winter winds sweep the snow from the plateau and expose forage. The cliffs on the north side of the plateau offer shelter from the violent storms as well as protected sites for spring lambing.

Late in the spring, the sheep begin their annual migration to the west. Crossing Rock Creek, they thread their way through four passes along the crest of the Beartooth Range, descending the slopes of the upper Clarks Fork north of Cooke City. Most of the ewes and lambs cross the Beartooth Highway and ascend the slopes of Pilot and Index peaks to spend the summer in the meadows of the Absaroka mountains, more than thirty circuitous miles from the winter range. Some of the rams enter the Absaroka Mountains; others continue to the west to summer in the mountains northwest of Cooke City. They may be seen on Cutoff Mountain in Slough Creek, and on Wolverine Mountain, Henderson Mountain, and Mount Abundance. There, they socialize with sheep from the West Rosebud herd.

A decade ago, the Rock Creek herd was an order of magnitude larger, Unfortunately, a storm in April 1991 decimated this herd.

The herd of some twenty-five sheep that winter on the Stillwater River near Mouat have been intensively studied in recent years because of mining in the Stillwater Complex. This herd was stressed by competition from livestock, but in 1967 a fence was built in cooperation with the owners of the Beartooth Ranch. The sheep fared well for a while, but have declined due to a variety of stresses on their winter range.

The Stillwater rams commonly pasture in the Monument Peak-Sheepherder Peak area near Independence. Ewes seem to summer along the Stillwater River and its eastern tributaries—Flood and Wounded Man creeks—near the Two Sisters, Cathedral Peak and Tumble Mountain.

The third herd, about fifty bighorns, winters in the West Rosebud in the vicinity of the Mystic Lake power station. Migrations of these sheep to their summer ranges are poorly understood. Ewes from this herd have been observed in the headwaters of Woodbine and Falls creeks, tributaries to the Stillwater River, and as far to the southwest as Cutoff Mountain in Slough Creek. On Cutoff Mountain, Wolverine Peak, Mount Abundance and Henderson and Miller mountains, they mix with the Rock Creek Herd. They also mix with the Druid Peak herd from Yellowstone National Park. Most of the adult rams and some of the ewes summer around Twin Peaks, Mount Wood and Mount Hague.

Although each Beartooth bighorn apparently belongs to one of the three distinct herds that winter in the same places every year, there is considerable scattering of sheep in the summer. They may be seen as far west as the high peaks at the headwaters of Hellroaring Creek and Buffalo Fork.

ROCKY MOUNTAIN GOATS

No animal better symbolizes the rugged alpine peaks and cliffs than the Rocky Mountain goat (*Oreamnos americanus*).

At the turn of the 20th century, the natural range of the mountain goats extended into the high country of northwestern Montana, but goats were probably restricted to west of the Continental Divide. Several mountain ranges east of the divide had suitable habitat, but because goats seldom venture into valleys between ranges, it would have taken decades, perhaps centuries, for the animals to reach the Beartooth.

In the early 1940s, the Montana Fish and Game Department decided to speed things up a bit by establishing a trapping and transplant program. In 1941, the first goats were released in the Crazy Mountains. The following year, twelve goats were transplanted in the Rock Creek drainage south of Red Lodge. Over the years, about sixty goats have been released in the Beartooth Mountains, in the drainages of Rock creek, the East Rosebud, the Stillwater, and Pine Creek, south of Livingston.

The initial stocking of twelve goats in Rock Creek took hold tenuously. In 1947, the herd was estimated at ten, but the presence of kids indicated successful reproduction. By 1955 a population had been established on the Line Creek Plateau to the southeast. It has continued to expand into Wyoming and now occupies Littlerock Creek and the Clarks Fork Canyon. In the Cooke City area, goats frequently are seen on Meridian Peak, Henderson, Miller and Scotch Bonnet mountains, as well as the peaks in the northeastern corner of Yellowstone National Park.

Between 1948 and 1956, about twenty-seven goats were released near the mouth of the East Rosebud Canyon. By the 1970s the herd numbered more than 70 and inhabited the high plateaus from Silver Run in the east to the Stillwater Plateau in the west. A favorite goat haunt is Froze-to-Death Plateau, where they are frequently observed by climbers en route to Granite Peak.

In 1945 and 1946 a few goats were released

along the main Stillwater River near Woodbine Camp. These goats, or their progeny, apparently migrated to the west and established a thriving population in the peaks from Independence to the west, along the divides of Slough Creek, Buffalo Fork, Hellroaring Creek, the Boulder River, and Mill Creek.

Pine Creek, south of Livingston, was the site of goat releases in 1957 and 1958. Today, goats can be seen in the crags around Marten Peak, and the multiple towers of Mount Cowen, as well as north as far as Livingston Peak.

Because of the success of the herd, the Montana Fish and Game Commission began to allow hunting of goats in 1960. By the 1970s, Fish and Game biologists could count more than 300 goats in the Beartooth Mountains and in 1975, fifty animals were taken. However, through the 1970s, the goat population showed a drastic decrease in the ratio of kids to adults, indicating poor reproduction. The reasons for the decline are a puzzle. Recent success and expansion of goats have raised concerns about their impact on alpine plant communities.

BEARTOOTH ALPINE BIRDS

Birds visiting the Beartooth Plateau seldom stay long. Trees are few, thus perches and shelters are scarce. Because of the short, cold growing season, vegetation production is limited and food is scant. It's just plain tough to raise a family in the alpine.

A few hardy birds breed and nest on the Beartooth plateau: golden eagle, prairie falcon, cliff swallow, horned lark, common raven, rock wren, mountain bluebird, robin, American pipit, Savannah sparrow, Lincoln's sparrow, white-crowned sparrow, American black rosy finch, and perhaps lesser scaup and Say's phoebe. Of these,

most also breed in other kinds of places, but the American pipit and the black rosy finch breed exclusively in the alpine.

The American pipit (formerly called water pipit) is probably the most common alpine bird on the Beartooth Plateau. They arrive with the spring, before it's easy for people to reach the heights, and immediately begin shopping for nesting sites. Sometimes the nest is secondhand, but it's always sunk into the ground and partially overhung by sod vegetation or a rock. Frost hummocks, which can provide shelter from prevailing winds, are popular homes.

After laying a clutch, which averages five eggs, the female incubates for about fourteen days and is fed by the male. Chicks are altricial (born with closed eyes and needing protection and care from the adults) and remain in the nest for another fourteen days. Then, after a week of straying from the nest, they are independent.

Though American pipits are plain-looking, they are easily identifiable. White outer tail feathers are visible in flight. The habit of bobbing their heads and tails while at rest is their most distinguishing characteristic.

Adult American pipits feed exclusively on insects, harvested from alpine meadows or nearby snow fields. Nature graciously blows the bugs onto the snowy surfaces where they are conveniently refrigerated. Competition for food is minimal, as the white-crowned sparrows and rosy finches rely heavily on seeds.

With the onset winter, as early as September, American pipits migrate to lower elevations and are commonly seen in fields, along streams, and near the ocean.

Rosy finches, more social and warier of people than are the American pipits, congregate in flocks that are easily startled. Rosy finches are also eas-

ily identified. Mostly black, they have a gray cap and washes of pink on their bellies, rumps, flanks, and wings. Ornithologists are considering splitting the species into two: black (which breeds in the alpine Beartooth) and gray-crowned.

Early in the spring rosy finches ascend the mountains from wintering grounds on lower slopes and valleys. Nest sites are chosen in rocky crevices or among boulders, then made comfortable with grass, hair, feathers, and moss.

Like American pipits, rosy finches lay about five eggs and incubate them for fourteen days. After living nest-bound for twenty days, the young join the adults and spend the rest of the summer in small flocks. Late in the fall, they migrate to lower elevations.

American pipits and rosy finches are part of the complexion and personality of the alpine. But it would be a mistake to portray that they are the only denizens of this open region. Other birds regularly nest there, and many others are regular visitors. Among these are the raptors that begin hunting in the alpine in the late summer when the young of marmots and ground squirrels are abundant. They also prey on insects and mature and immature birds.

A list of the birds observed on the alpine Beartooth Plateau is included in the Appendix.

FISH

To many, the essence of the Beartooth is its fishery. Fish abound in the thousand lakes splashed across the plateau and in the hundreds of miles of streams that tumble from the heights to the plains.

The plenitude of fish is unique to the 20th century. Because most Beartooth streams are too steep to allow spawners to ascend and because cascades isolate most of the lakes, very few of the moun-

Above: Cliff swallows.
Left top: Golden eagle.
Left: Male mountain bluebird.

Facing page, top left: Brown trout.
Top right: A Thompson Lake catch.
Bottom left: Grayling.
Bottom right: Cutthroat trout.

JOHN LAMBING

GEORGE WUERTHNER

GEORGE WUERTHNER

PAUL VUCETICH

tain waters supported fish before white people arrived. For the most part, the fishery of the Beartooth was limited to the lower reaches of the streams.

There were a few exceptions. Lake Abundance, near Cooke City, was reported by Bart Henderson to be teeming with trout when visited by his band of prospectors in 1870.

As early as the 1920s, local miners, packers, rod and gun club members, and government agents began to carry fish to the mountains so they could carry them out later. These fish, it was hoped, would establish reproducing populations or simply grow into lunkers. Transplants, in buckets and pails, were carried on foot and on horseback, and later with aircraft.

In the eastern part of the range, brook trout were supplied to the Red Lodge Rod and Gun Club by the National Fish Hatchery at Bozeman. The fry were held in ponds at Richel Lodge and allocated to club members for distribution.

Many of the early transplants survived. Subsequently, the Montana Fish and Game Department got serious and systematic about the program. Long before there was much understanding of the limnology of alpine waters and the positive and negative effects of fish-stocking, a third of the Beartooth's lakes had been planted.

Fish planting was done without regard for the needs of the planted fish and the characteristics of the receiving waters. The reproductive potentials of lakes were ignored, as were the requirements of spawning fish. And fish were planted without regard to the effect on preexisting fisheries, either in the receiving water or downstream. Mistakes were made. Some lakes were overstocked and many small-sized fish populations with little appeal to anglers were created.

About 35 percent of the Beartooth's lakes have

fisheries. Forty percent of the lake waters have virtually no potential for establishing a fishery. As for the streams, many in the Beartooth are important as nurseries and food producers, but few in the higher elevations have resident fisheries.

The waters of the Beartooth are generally considered oligotrophic (poor producers because of low nutrient concentrations). In addition, they tend to have low temperatures and short growing seasons. Therefore, one would conclude, they should have poor fisheries.

Indeed, compared with low-elevation waters, Beartooth lakes are low in nutrients and have short, cold growing seasons. However, many of these lakes are generally free from pollution and other human-caused disturbances. Their clear waters allow good penetration of light energy and they have stable water levels. Finally, they often have excellent morphological features (shapes). The semiannual overturnings experienced by many of them causes a healthy exchange of nutrients and oxygen between the waters at different depths. The result can be very diverse and productive fisheries.

The most common fish in the high country of the Beartooth is the brook trout (*Salvelinus fontinalis*), which inhabits about 13 percent of the lakes. Widely available in the early years of planting, they reproduce well in cold fall waters with low levels. Early spring emergence after a long incubation gives them an initial growth advantage.

Other species found in the Beartooth, in order of relative abundance, are: cutthroats (*Salmo clarki*), rainbows (*Oncorhynchus mykiss*), grayling (*Thymallus arcticus*), and goldens (*Oncorhynchus aquabonita*). Lake chubs (*Couesius plumbeus*) found their way into Lake Abundance but were

poisoned in 1970 because of their adverse effect on the cutthroat population. Some Beartooth streams, for example the West Rosebud, have healthy populations of brown trout (*Salmo trutta*). Mountain whitefish (*Prosopium williamsoni*) and longnose suckers (*Cataotomus catostomus*) are found at lower elevations in streams. White suckers (*Castostomus commersoni*) inhabit East Rosebud Lake.

The most beautiful and least common fish of the Beartooth is the golden trout, a California native indigenous only to the Cottonwood Lakes and a few tributaries of the Kern River. Goldens were introduced in Montana in 1907 and were planted in about thirty mountain lakes over a thirty-year period. In 1938, the first plant in the Beartooth was made. The export of golden trout eggs was banned by the state of California in 1939, so its further propagation will be limited, although at least one lake in the Beartooth has produced fingerlings that have been taken to other locations. Once, a golden estimated to weigh ten to twelve pounds was trapped by a researcher. A 4.9-pound, 22½-inch Beartooth beauty set the Montana state angling record in 1993.

About a dozen lakes in the Beartooth have golden trout and several others have hybrids of golds and rainbows or cutthroats. Distribution of golden trout in the Beartooth is extremely limited because of the precise spawning requirements of the fish. Where goldens are successful, they are very long-lived. In one Beartooth lake, where spawning was not successful, fourteen-year-old goldens were found.

The arctic grayling, know for a spectacular dorsal fin, is a northern latitude species once found also in northern Michigan, but now found in the lower forty-eight states only in Montana. Lewis and Clark wrote of grayling in the entire drainage of the Missouri River above the Great Falls, but it is now limited to about twenty-five mountain lakes on both sides of the Continental Divide, and in small stretches of the Sun, Big Hole, Red Rock, and Madison rivers. Its numbers have declined to the point that threatened status is being proposed.

The largest grayling ever taken in Montana was a 2½-pounder from Georgetown Lake. The largest ever netted in the Beartooth weighed about 2¼ pounds. Conservationists have requested that the grayling be protected under the federal endangered species act.

Perhaps the most popular fish of the Beartooth is the cutthroat trout, or "native." Although normally they grow to only about 2½ pounds in this region, they are colorful, feisty, and delicious. Once found in all of the streams in and adjacent to the mountains of Montana and Wyoming, the cutthroat is now limited to the headwaters, and even this shrunken range is threatened.

Sensitive to its environment, the cutthroat demands unpolluted water and competes poorly with brook and brown trout. Because its spawning habits are similar to those of the rainbows, hybridization is common where the species coexist.

Most cutthroats in the Beartooth high lakes are descendants of a pure strain that originated in McBride Lake (in Slough Creek) and propagated at a Big Timber hatchery. An exception is Goose Lake near Cooke City, which has reproducing cutthroats with characteristics identified as pure Yellowstone. Although the origin of these fish cannot be verified, one tale is that Bud Hart, who had a cabin at the outlet of Goose Lake in 1906 and 1907, carried pails of "cutts" from the Clarks Fork River to the Lake.

In addition to the outstanding high lake fishery, many Beartooth streams are nationally renowned: the Yellowstone, the Boulder, and the Stillwater. Less famous streams offer excellent angling due to robust discharges, gentle gradients, good cover, and abundant food. Slough Creek, Rock Creek, Buffalo Fork, Hellroaring (the one that flows south into Yellowstone National Park), and Mill Creek are but a few.

The practice of indiscriminate fish planting has been retired. In its place is a policy based on the habitat needs of the fish and the effects of the fish on its waters. It also recognizes that the presence of game fish in a wilderness lake or stream can have the adverse effect of attracting too much human use to a sensitive environment and can destroy a vanishing resource—wilderness solitude. Because solitude and fish rarely coexist, wilderness managers and users alike are beginning to rethink wilderness water management policies. No longer is it blindly accepted that every lake with suitable habitat for fish should have fish (or names, for that matter).

It is worthwhile to keep fish from some suitable waters to enhance research on the ecology of other organisms in the lake. Better fish management and recreational fishing can result.

Plants of the Alpine World

On the Beartooth Plateau, spring lasts all summer. The high elevation and the many protected north-facing cirques and slopes ensure that there are always wet meadows that have recently emerged from the snow. The visual harvest of these meadows is a continuous splash of color, much of it from cushion plants: white flowering phlox and smelowskia, pink douglasia and dwarf alpine clover, sparkling blue alpine forget-me-not, purple pasque flowers, yellow avens, biscuit-root and mountain buttercups.

The first detailed scientific studies of the alpine vegetation of the Beartooth Plateau were conducted in 1962 by P.L. Johnson and Dwight Billings, who collected 210 different species of vascular plants. But the Beartooth Plateau is only one of a dozen separate, large, high plateaus in the Beartooth Range, which has a greater expanse of alpine vegetation than any other mountain range of the Montana Rockies. Although recent collections have increased the number of plant species found on the Beartooth Plateau to 422, much of the high country in the Beartooth remains botanically unexplored.

In the northwestern part of the range, on the East and West Boulder plateaus, several plants of northwestern origin and distribution are com-

JOHN REDDY

mon: mountain heath (*Phyllodoce*), mountain heather (*Cassiope*), and the alpine St. Johns-wort (*Hypericum formosum* var. *nortoniae*). On a single limestone outcrop, two well known calciocoles (plants occurring only on limestone soils) have been collected: the fragrant cream-colored androsace (*Androsace lehmanniana*), and the dwarf blue columbine (*Aquilegia jonesii*).

Many partly or wholly circumpolar, arctic-alpine plants occur in the Beartooth Mountains. Of these, some are not known from collections taken elsewhere in Montana: the dwarf alpine annual Iceland plant (*Koenigia islandica*), icegrass (*Phippsia algida*), twice-hairy butterweed (*Senecio fuscatus*), goat saxifrage (*Saxifraga hirenhis*), cotton grass (*Eriophorum callitoix*), bighead kobresia (*Kobresia macrocarga*) and arctic rush (*Juncus triglmis* var. *triglumus*).

An endemic is a plant whose range is confined to a single restricted area. No known plants are Beartooth Range endemics. However, a few plants found in the Beartooth alpine area are endemic to southwestern Montana, northwestern Wyoming, and adjacent Idaho (the Greater Yellowstone ecosystem, more or less):

Palish larkspur (*Delphinium glaucescens*)

Purple crazyweed (*Oxytropis besseyi*, var. *argophylla*)

Above: Magenta-colored monkeyflowers carpet a stream.
Right top: Aspen and wild roses on East Rosebud Creek.
Right: Fireweed in the Lake Plateau region.
Facing page: Lupine

Rabbit-foot crazyweed (*Oxytropis lagopus*, var. *atropurpurea*)

Hayden's clover (*Trifolium haysenii*)

Snow paintbrush (*Castilleja nivea*)

Fern-leaved lousewort (*Pedicularis cystopterideafolia*)

Pretty dwarf lousewort (*Pedicularis pulchella*)

Tweedy's thistle (*Cirsium tweedyii*)

Fan-leaved daisy (*Erigeron flabellifolius*)

Slender fleabane (*Erigeron gracilis*)

Rydberg's daisy (*Erigeron rydbergii*)

The alpine flora of the Beartooth Mountains appears to be richer than that of any other North American mountain range. Why is the Beartooth flora so rich? Many explanations have been offered.

The Rocky Mountain ranges with the richest floras are the high ones that trend east and west and intersect the principal north-south ranges. Examples are the Uintas in Utah and the San Juans of Colorado and New Mexico. And the Beartooth in Montana and Wyoming. The north slopes of these east-west ranges receive little direct sunshine through the summer, resulting in slow runoff, late snow beds and development of swamps, bogs, and lakes at high elevations.

Many plants in the high mountains are circumpolar—distributed all around the world in the high latitudes—and have invaded the mountainous areas to the south. The east-west trending mountain ranges have been successful at intersecting the movements of these plants.

The richness of the Beartooth flora may also be an indirect result of the height of the range. Over millions of years, the climate of the world has undergone drastic changes. For millennia, the climate in North America was tropical. Then, about a million years ago, in the early Cenozoic era, the climate cooled and glaciers covered much of the landscape, destroying the tropical plants and altering their habitat. Because of its height, the Beartooth range was not entirely glaciated. The high peaks remained ice-free, as did a few other "refugia." A few species of plants that had lived in the region during a warmer time were able to survive. During the Altithermal Period (a warm drought, 4,000 to 7,000 years ago) north-facing slopes had arctic-like conditions, and again were refugia for arctic and alpine plants.

The copiousness of the Beartooth flora may also have been influenced by the expansiveness of the alpine terrain. Other states, notably Colorado, have higher elevations, but perhaps no other U.S. mountain range south of Alaska has as much land above the treeline. The several hundred thousand acres of alpine Beartooth plateau and its plethora of north-facing cirques, alpine bogs and meadows constitute a nonpareil environment for botanical diversity.

Geological factors have been important in the Beartooth formula of vegetation as well. Most of the Beartooth Plateau consists of crystalline rocks such as granite. These rocks weather into a soil with a characteristic makeup of nutrients with low concentrations of lime and its related carbonate minerals. Some plants are suited to these soils, but others prefer soils richer in carbonates that weather from limestone. Limestone soils exist in the Beartooth, for example on Clay and Beartooth buttes, and in many places on the periphery of the range where the sedimentary rocks are draped over the edges of uplifted crystalline rocks. Many calcicoles are found in such soils.

The Red Lodge-Cooke City highway has contributed to the perception of floral diversity in the alpine of the Beartooth. Built in the 1930s, this road offers easy access to the plateau and its organic carpet. More is known about the vegetation near this highway than that of most other Montana alpine areas. Knowledge of alpine vegetation has followed highway construction elsewhere: Logan Pass, on Going-to-the-Sun Highway in Glacier National Park, and Trail Ridge in Rocky Mountain National Park, Colorado.

Several plants associated with the southern and central Rocky Mountains are found in the Beartooth: golden saxifrage (*Saxifraga crysantha flavum*), alpine poppy (*Papaver*), Colorado columbine (*Aquilegia coerulea*), and several clovers (*Trifolium dasyphyllum*, *T. nanum*, and *T. parryi*).

Other Beartooth plants are more commonly associated with the western part of Montana or the Pacific Northwest. The western side of the Beartooth, in particular the northwestern corner, has a climate not unlike that of Montana's western ranges. Although Paradise Valley is extremely dry, the mountains to the east of the valley represent the eastern or southern limits of several plants. Beargrass (*Xerophyllum tenax*), common in northwestern Montana but rare east of the Continental Divide, occurs here, as do the mooseberry (*Viburnum edule*), white spruce (*Picea glauca*), western white pine (*Pinus monticola*), and western trillium (*Trillium ovatum*), which is common to the boreal region of Canada and the northwestern United States.

On the Wyoming portion of the plateau, several alpine bog habitats may have served as refugia during the extensive glaciation of the Montana portion of the plateau to the north. These bogs, often found in association with permafrost within three feet of the surface, are similar to wetlands in the Arctic.

The terms "tundra" and "arctic-alpine" are often used to describe the high, open ecosystem of the plateau. The similarity in appearance between the alpine and the tundra is obvious, and fully half of the plant species found in the Beartooth alpine flora also occur in the Arctic. In contrast, only 10 to 15 percent of the plants of the Sierra Nevada alpine are found in the Arctic.

There are, however, significant differences between the "arctic" and the "alpine." In general, the alpine is a harsher environment; it experiences more wind, less vapor pressure, lower surface soil temperatures, high ultraviolet radiation, less soil moisture, and greater diurnal temperature fluctuations. The most significant similarity between the alpine and the arctic is the short, cold growing season. Thus, the term "tundra" is reserved by many authors for the Arctic lowlands.

The most striking trait of the alpine landscape is the scarcity of trees. The few that survive acquire forms conspicuously different from those of lower elevations. Instead of being tall and symmetrical they are stunted, often flagged by the wind, and gregarious, seemingly huddled together for protection against the elements. This is the "Krummholz" or crooked-wood ecosystem.

"Alpine," a concept without precise definition, generally, means above timberline. But the term "timberline" is not precise. Timberline is not a line, but a zone. The alpine may be defined as the area in the high mountains (as opposed to the Arctic) that is devoid of trees. Several forces, often acting together, hinder tree growth in the high elevations. Among them are excessive wind, low carbon dioxide vapor pressure, deep snow, desiccation during cold weather, deficient heat, and intense light.

Amid the occasional spartan trees one sees the brilliant colors of the alpine flowers. Close inspection reveals a rich mosaic of vegetation. Inspections must be close indeed. This mosaic of interwoven flora, of minuscule alpine vegetation,

is a Middle Earth, where plants are dwarves and hobbits. Inspections of the floral carpet may be fruitful only when the observer sets eyeball to earth. The usual erect posture of the *Homo sapiens* cannot provide the proximity necessary to view each tiny biological wonder.

We tend to think of this environment as harsh and, in human terms, it is. But alpine plants, not having to pass the productivity tests of economic exploitation, thrive on it. They live here because they are suited to it.

Suited to what? What are the characteristics of the alpine environment? The most obvious is the role of the physical environment, which is altered little by the biological one, as it is in a forest. Radiation and wind strongly affect temperature and the distribution of snow and its meltwater. Permafrost—permanently frozen ground—and cycles of freezing and thawing heave the soil, strongly affecting the patterns of plants.

During the few fleeting summer and fall afternoons when air temperatures reach the seventies or eighties, the vegetation makes the best of the heat. More often, summer temperatures are low and overnight frost is common. Winter is never far away and snow covers much of the landscape much of the time.

The alpine environment is characterized by extreme fluctuations in the energy budget. Because of high elevation and, therefore, less atmospheric absorption of the sun's rays, the radiation input on clear summer days is brutally high. On clear nights, the loss of energy can freeze a large 10,000-foot-high lake, even in the warmest part of the summer. Since stress from cold and drought is common in the alpine, plants that live there must be hardy. Mechanisms for survival include decreased water potential, high concentrations of soluble carbohydrates, and closed stomates.

Many alpine plants are prostrate—even woody species like willows. They are typically perennial, since completing an entire life cycle—from germination to flower to seed—in a single, short, cold season is possible for but a handful of plants. Of the 422 species that have been collected from the Beartooth alpine, only ten can be considered annuals:

Thick-leaved draba (*Draba crassifolia*). Normally a winter annual, often biennial and sometimes a short-lived perennial.

Slender draba (*Draba stenoloba*). Winter annual, very rarely becoming biennial.

Yellowcress (*Rorippa obtusa* var. *alpina*). Winter annual, often biennial, sometimes short-lived perennial.

Iceland plant (*Koenigia islandica*). The only true annual in the Beartooth alpine zone.

Douglas' knotweed (*Polygonum douglasii*). Annual and/or winter annual, not known in the Beartooth to exist longer than for one season.

Englemann's knotweed (*Polygonum englmannii*). Annual and/or winter annual, not known in the Beartooth to exist longer than for one season.

Leafy dwarf knotweed (*Polygonum minimum*). Annual and/or winter annual, not known in the Beartooth to exist longer than for one season.

Fairy candelabra (*Androsace septenrionalis*). Winter annual, often biennial and not too uncommon as a short-lived perennial.

Moss gentian (*Gentiana prostrata*). Believed to be a winter annual and not to persist for another season.

Some species that are annuals in lower elevations may be biennials in the alpine. Fairy candelabra (*Androsace septenrionalis*) is an example.

Alpine plants tend to develop most—up to 85 percent—of their bulk underground. Only the essential parts—the leaves for photosynthesis and

Clockwise from right:
Paintbrush and Lupine.
Beargrass.
Mariposa (or Sego) lily.
Paintbrush.
Snow willow.

Above: *Wood lily on East Rosebud Creek.*
Top: *Arrowleaf balsamroot along Sage Creek.*
Left: *Waterleaf.*
Far left: *Asters, buttercups, lupines (and more) in the Island Lakes area.*

the flowers for reproduction—grow above the surface. Woody stems are unneeded for support and energy storage takes place in large root or rhizome systems.

Alpine plants have metabolic systems that are able to capture, store and utilize energy at low temperatures and over brief periods. Energy can be reserved until conditions are suitable for growth of leaves and flowers.

Pollination is a tenuous process for high elevation plants. Because temperatures are usually low, pollen transport by insect activity is limited to the few warm afternoons. Even so, insects, especially the short-tongued bees, bumblebees, flies, butterflies, and moths, are important. Long-tubed flowers, such as the arctic gentian (*Gentiana algida*), are pollinated by the bumblebees, while the flatter, more open blossoms are visited by a variety of flies. Some pollination is accomplished by the wind and by birds.

Close inspection will also reveal that the alpine environment is not as uniform as it first appears. The topography changes as it grades from the high windward slopes to the ridge tops, the leeward snow, the meltwater meadows, and the bogs. Along this gradient a few plants, like the yellow avens (*Geum rossi*), can be found from one end to the other. But most species are restricted to certain segments due to the drastic variation in moisture and temperature along the gradient.

Many tap-rooted cushion plants and dwarf rosette forbs with deep roots are found on the exposed and dry windward slopes and ridge tops. On the upper leeward slopes, moist from the winter accumulation of snow, vegetation tends to be open and represented by perennial forbs and bunch grasses. Below the snowbanks, in the west meadows, are luxuriant stands of sedges, grasses, and wet-site dicots.

Each of the Beartooth's alpine plateaus is an island or a peninsula, separated from the others by deep, glaciated canyons. Each, therefore, has had an opportunity to develop its own flora. The plateaus have botanical similarities, to be sure, and, at a glance they all seem alike, but each has a singular floral makeup and distribution, and each harbors different dominant species.

Plants have been collected on the plateaus for more than a century. F.V. Hayden made several trips to the Yellowstone Park area, beginning in 1871. In 1871, Hayden traveled to the New World Mining District near present-day Cooke City and visited Daisy Pass, the head of the Stillwater River, and Lake Abundance.

Perhaps the first plant collection taken from the plateau was by Dr. W.H. Forwood, a surgeon who accompanied Lt. Gen. Phillip Sheridan in 1881 and 1882. Forwood collected nearly 300 species from the Wind River Range to the Clarks Fork of the Yellowstone River, but perusal of his list and reports of the trip reveals that Sheridan hastened across the Beartooth Plateau, allowing Forwood little time to collect and observe. Few plants were collected on the plateau and many common ones are conspicuous by their absence from his list.

Montana's most active plant collector prior to the 20th century was Frank Tweedy, an amateur botanist and author of short stories, who was a U.S.G.S. topographer by profession. In the early 1880s he participated in the first topographic survey of southern Montana and Yellowstone National Park, as well as the Beartooth Mountains. His Yellowstone Park collections, including representation from Slough and Soda Butte creeks on the southern face of the Beartooth were published in 1886 as *Flora of the Yellowstone National Park*. In 1887 he collected intensely, logging specimens from Mill Creek, the West Boulder River, the East Boulder River, Hellroaring Creek, Deep Creek, Haystack Peak, the East Boulder and West Boulder plateaus, Davis Creek, and the Stillwater Canyon, Grizzly Creek, Bear Gulch, Emigrant Gulch, and the Boulder River.

In 1897 and 1899, Peter Koch of Bozeman collected plants on horseback trips to Cooke City and Yellowstone National Park via the Boulder River. His collections include plants from the Lake Plateau and from the Granite Range (that part of the Beartooth near Granite Peak).

P.A. Rydberg, curator of the herbarium of the New York Botanical Garden, collected in Montana in the late 1890s. In 1897, accompanied by Ernst A. Bessey, he visited the Mill Creek and Emigrant Gulch area south of Livingston. Among his many publications was the *Flora of Montana and the Yellowstone National Park*, issued in 1900. The collections of Koch, Rydberg, and, especially Tweedy, gave species of the Beartooth excellent representation in this catalog of Montana plants.

Also in 1897, E.V. Wilcox collected in the western part of the Beartooth for the U.S. Department of Agriculture.

Pliny Hawkins came to Columbus, Montana, in 1894 at age twenty-five to be the only teacher in a temporary school. Before long he was named principal of the permanent school built to educate the children of a growing community. An avid student of natural history, he often prospected and explored in the Beartooth Mountains, eager to learn to identify minerals, plants and animals. From 1900 to 1902, he collected plants from the Beartooth Plateau and was awarded a master's degree in botany from Montana State College (now MSU) in 1903. His thesis topic: the alpine flora of Montana.

Hawkins founded the Columbus State Bank

and served as its cashier, dispensed wisdom as justice of the peace, platted the town of Absarokee, and prospered as a real estate developer. In 1920 he donated the land for what is now Hawkins Parks so local folks could have access to the Rosebud River. In 1923 he published a series of articles titled "Native Flowers and Trees" in the *Absaroka Enterprise*. In 1924 he published *The Trees and Shrubs of Yellowstone National Park*.

J.B. Leiberg, a forester employed by the Northern Pacific Railroad and later by the U.S. Geological Survey, surveyed the resources of the Absaroka Forest Reserve. His monograph *Forest Conditions in the Absaroka Division of the Yellowstone Forest Reserve, Montana and the Livingston and Big Timber Quadrangles* was published in 1904.

The plants of the Absaroka-Beartooth have been observed and collected off and on since the turn of the 20th century, reaching an apex with the work of Johnson and Billings. K.H. Lackschewitz, the dean of Montana alpine botanists, has compiled an exhaustive list of the species collected in the alpine of the Beartooth of Montana and Wyoming. His list, heretofore unpublished, appears at the back of this book. Peter Lesica has collected extensively on the Line Creek plateau and found many species not previously reported from the Beartooth; they have been added to the Lackschewitz list.

PINK SNOW

The title of Maurice Fitzgerald's 1960 film, *Land of the Pink Snow*, publicized a phrase often used since to describe the Beartooth Mountains. Although not unique to the Beartooth, pink snow is common there because of the vast expanse of high elevation landscape and the concomitant accumulations of snow. At times the snowbanks are intensely pink and orange. Other times, the surface color is subtle, but indentations, such as footprints, may be blood-red from the compaction of pigmented cells.

Colored snow fascinated Aristotle and has intrigued scientists for centuries. In the late 1900s, it was recognized that the reds and other colors often seen in mountain snows are from blooms of microscopic algae. More than 100 species (sixty in the United States) have been recognized. The most common and widely distributed species, that of the "pink snow" in the Beartooth, is *Chlamydomonas nivalis*.

The alpine snowfield is a self-contained ecosystem. At the base of the food chain are the algae, which grow and reproduce by combining energy from the sun with dissolved nutrients and carbon dioxide. In summer, the colored pigments of the algae absorb and hold energy and increase the temperature of the cells. "Sun cups," slight depressions in the snow, have high concentrations of algae. Grazing on these single-celled plants is a variety of creatures, many of them microscopic: protozoans, ciliates, nematodes, spiders, rotifers, springtails, and snowworms. Slim, black, snake-like snowworms, about an inch long, wriggle across the surface of the snow. Dining on them (and on wind-deposited insects) are the alpine birds—American pipits, horned larks, and rosy finches.

Birds remove much biomass from the snow, but they leave something just as important—nutrients, in the form of droppings. Wind-borne pollen, insects, and leaf litter lodge in the snow and provide supplemental nutrient after bacterial decomposition.

One key step in the annual cycle of the snowfield ecosystem is the "reseeding" of colored algae at the snow surface. This may be accomplished by the wind, by birds, or even by the algae themselves. Experiments with *Chlamydomonas nivalis* indicate that the cells winter in the soil beneath the snow. In the spring, when the temperature and the light are just right, resting spores produce flagellated cells that swim upward through the snowpack to the surface. Thus, the circle is complete.

WILDERNESS: AN UNCERTAIN FUTURE

When President Jimmy Carter signed the Absaroka-Beartooth wilderness bill on March 27, 1978, an era of controversy ended. Wilderness supporters and conservationists breathed a sigh of accomplishment, and development advocates gritted their teeth in anger or resignation. Ostensibly laid to rest were disputes over proposals for a road through Slough Creek, and several timber sales. Over 900,000 acres of the Beartooth uplift had been preserved in a wild condition for future generations.

But many of the controversies haven't died. They have merely changed their flavor. Since the bill's passage, threats to the integrity of the wilderness have ranged from proposals for large mines on the periphery of the wilderness to a 300-foot-high statue of Christ on Beartooth Pass.

The statue has gone looking for a better site, and the Slough Creek road was mortally wounded. The wilderness bill specifically recognized the legal controversy over the road and pointedly evaded it: "Nothing in this act shall be construed as affecting in any manner or to any extent any claim by Park County, Montana and Sweet Grass County, Montana, to a right-of-way from Cooke City, Montana, to Boulder." As recently as the early 1990s, both counties petitioned the U.S. Forest Service for a road. The Forest Service Northern Region solicitor denied the claim.

Congress already made a "boundary adjustment" to the Absaroka-Beartooth Wilderness. At Passage Creek, a tributary to Mill Creek, on the west side of the wilderness, the boundary was altered, deleting twenty-seven acres from the Wilderness, to allow a road to be built to a subdivided inholding, even though the wilderness act allows for reasonable access to private land.

Another proposed adjustment has been resisted. Sprawling, alpine Goose Lake near Cooke City overlies a zone of mineralized rock that has been probed and explored since the turn of the 20th century or

GEORGE ROBBINS

RICK GRAETZ

BRUCE SELYEM

GEORGE ROBBINS

Above: From just below the summit of Challis Peak and above Wounded Man Lake.
Left: Elk Lake.
Far left top: Gardiner Lake, just over the border in Wyoming, along the Beartooth Highway.
Far left: Reminder of human presence on the ruggedly beautiful land.

Facing page: Lone Mountain's coat of trees includes whitebark pine and subalpine fir.

91

before. No discoveries have been economical to mine, but many claims have been staked and a few have been patented. The Copper King Mining Company, owner of the claims, opposed inclusion of Goose Lake inside the wilderness boundary and, from time to time, asked for a 2,000-acre deletion.

The purposeful inclusion of Goose Lake in the Wilderness by Congress recognized both the mineral potential and the fragile nature of the landscape. If mining is to be done, as is allowed on valid claims in designated wilderness, it should be done with the protection of the surface that the wilderness act provides. An important principle is at stake here. How permanent, how secure is wilderness protection? Will Congress, at the request of developers, delete significant acreage from wilderness?

Snowmobilers feel disadvantaged by the wilderness designation. They believe they leave no trace, have no impact on vegetation and wildlife, and are compatible with other, nonmechanized recreation like cross-country skiing. They have pressed the Montana congressional delegation to either delete the Slough Creek corridor from the wilderness or make a snowmobile exemption. Wilderness trespass by snowmobilers in Slough Creek and in places around Cooke City is common.

As sweeping as the wilderness bill was, it failed to protect many deserving areas: the Wyoming high lakes, the Clarks Fork Canyon and River, the Line Creek Plateau, and the Deep Lake area.

The lake country south of the Montana-Wyoming border and north of the Beartooth Highway was not included in the original bill because of lack of support from the Wyoming congressional delegation. By 1984, Wyoming was ready. Congress enacted a Wyoming wilderness bill that protected 23,750 acres as wilderness and set aside 14,700 acres for wilderness study. The act set no deadline for the Secretary of Agriculture to submit a wilderness study recommendation to the president. The Forest Service planned to take up the matter as a part of the revision of the Shoshone Forest plan in the late 1990s. In the meantime, the study area is required to be managed so as not to diminish the wilderness resource. Snowmobiling and mountain biking are allowed.

In 1990, Congress enacted legislation protecting the undeveloped segment of the Clarks Fork River. The act designates 20.5 miles of river, from just below the Crandall Creek Bridge to just above the national forest boundary at the mouth of the canyon near Cyclone Bar, as "wild," the first such designation in Wyoming. Hydroelectric development in the canyon is precluded, but downstream development is not.

Between the Beartooth Highway and the Clarks Fork Canyon in Wyoming is the 75,000-acre Deep Lake area. Landslide-formed Deep Lake is spectacular. Even more spectacular is the canyon of the Clarks Fork Yellowstone River, which forms the southern edge of the Beartooth uplift and the proposed wilderness. Conservationists propose wilderness protection for this area.

Montana's Line Creek Plateau is contiguous with the Deep Lake area. It extends from the Beartooth Highway eastward toward the lip of the plateau and supports subalpine fir, Engelmann spruce, Douglas fir, and lodgepole pine forest that descends to the foothills. The heights of the Beartooth to the west intercept much of the moisture before it can reach this eastern extreme of the plateau. Therefore, the Line Creek Plateau is not as verdant as the plateau to the west and north. The Line Creek Plateau is a link in a continuum of impressive botanical diversity from the alpine of the Beartooth Plateau to the near-desert of the Clarks Fork river valley below. Conservationists propose wilderness protection for about 20,000 acres here, as well as designation of the Meeteetse Spires Preserve, a cooperative project of the Nature Conservancy, the Bureau of Land Management and private landowners.

Since about 1980, the Montana congressional delegation has tried to pass a Montana wilderness bill. In its mid-1990s incarnation it would add several small areas to the Absaroka-Beartooth Wilderness in order to improve the boundary, recognize important wilderness values, or resolve conflicts. These areas are: Timberline Creek and Burnt Mountain (both in the Lake Fork of Rock Creek); Mystic Lake; Mount Rae, Tie Creek and the north slopes of Livingston Peak; and the eastern slopes of Paradise Valley (roughly from Pine Creek to Mill Creek).

MINING ISSUES

In recent years, mining in the Beartooth has made a resurgence. Mines are operating at Jardine and Nye. A new mine was approved in the East Boulder. Exploration was done at Independence and Emigrant Gulch. A serious proposal for mining the New World District near Cooke City was advanced. In all cases, these mines or proposals threaten the resources of the nearby wilderness.

This frenetic activity has challenged the complex system for both resource development and environmental protection. At the heart of the issue is the mining law of 1872.

The Stillwater Complex, a world-class mineral deposit, was described early in this book, as were the recent mining developments there. The Stillwater Mining Company, a partnership of Manville and Chevron, won approval to mine platinum and palladium at the old Mouat site on the Stillwater. The mine, opened in 1986, was successful and the company obtained approval in 1992 to double the size of the operation, despite problems with nitrate pollution.

Stillwater Mining Company also explored the East Boulder part of the Stillwater Complex, eleven miles south of McLeod and thirty miles south of Big Timber, at elevations ranging from 6,200 to 9,250 feet. It sought approval to open an underground platinum and palladium mine, build a mill to process and concentrate the ore, and construct a tailing retention impoundment. Approval was granted in 1993.

Knowledge of mineralization in the gulch of Bear Creek dates to 1866, when Joe Brown found placer gold at the mouth of the creek. Underground mining, with accompanying milling and smelting, proceeded in earnest through the last part of the nineteenth century and well into the twentieth. By the 1920s most of the high-grade ore had been exhausted, but arsenic recovery kept the operation going until the late 1940s when a fire destroyed the cyanide mill and the federal government foreclosed on its loans.

In 1978 the Anaconda Company acquired the property and began serious exploring for gold. The Homestake Mining Company, well known for its deep gold mine at Lead, South Dakota, acquired the property in 1979 and continued to explore. Homestake formed a partnership with American Copper and Nickel Company in 1984; in 1988, the partners announced plans for a mine and went through the arduous process of winning government approval. Commercial production began in 1989 at a scale of 450 tons of ore per day. Although it can be seen from Mammoth Hot Springs in Yellowstone National Park, the mine has been a good citizen, living up to its environ-mental and community responsibilities. It was sold to a Canadian in 1993.

A contentious mining proposal emerged at the New World Mining District near Cooke City. At the heads of the Stillwater River, Soda Butte Creek (tributary to the Lamar River in Yellowstone National Park), and Fisher Creek (tributary to the Clarks Fork of the Yellowstone) at elevations ranging from 8,500 to 10,000 feet above sea level, a highly mineralized area has been extensively explored and mined in the past, as recently as the 1950s. Open pit mining at the McLaren Mine on Henderson Mountain left devastation that was an embarrassment to the mining industry of modern times. In Fisher Creek, acid (pH 2.9) gushing out of the adits sterilized the stream.

Crown Butte, Ltd., a subsidiary of the Canadian mining firm Noranda, envisioned a surface mine for low-grade ore and a cyanide leaching process. It found an unexpectedly high-grade gold deposit, estimated to be worth several hundred million dollars, which could be mined underground and processed without cyanide. It was the kind of lode miners dream about.

The company seemed to be taking enormous risks, however. The New World site is a scant two and one half miles from Yellowstone National Park and a mile and a half from the Absaroka-Beartooth Wilderness, in an alpine environment with serious water quality problems because of the acidic nature of the minerals and the carelessness of previous mining. Environmental groups dug in their heels, citing serious problems:

A tailings impoundment in Fisher Creek could threaten water quality in the wild Clarks Fork River. The blue-ribbon Stillwater River and Soda Butte Creek, which flows into Yellowstone National Park, could be threatened by mining activity nearby.

The mine would encroach on grizzly habitat. Yellowstone National Park is dangerously close. The mine would require a new power line to the site.

Montana would get the tax income, but Wyoming would bear much of the social impact.

Year-round trucking of ore to Cody, Wyoming, would impinge on recreation and moose habitat, and opening the road in the winter would increase traffic through Yellowstone National Park.

Conservationists appealed to political leaders. Montana Senator Max Baucus, Governor Mike Sullivan of Wyoming, the Environmental Protection Agency, and the National Park Service responded in varying degrees. Environmental groups turned also to the courts, asking the company to clean up not only its own mess, but also the one left by the miners who previously dug and ran.

At the bottom line, under the 1872 federal mining law and Montana state law, there is probably no insurmountable legal barrier to mining at a place like the New World District. The company, however, may not be able to cut through the barrier of public opinion and the cost of the associated hassle.

Lessons can be learned from the mineralization in the Beartooth. At their core is the proverbial mining axiom: you mine where the minerals are.

Yes, minerals are where they are, but that presence doesn't imply a right to mine. Minerals aren't inherently good or bad. They're marketplace products that benefit society in many ways, but which also have costs to society not counted in the calculus of the market; i.e., their price doesn't necessarily reflect their total cost.

Needed is a mining law that recognizes:

There is no inalienable right to mine.

The public interest should be considered in de-

Above: *The Stillwater Mine.*
Right top: *Noranda mining roads.*
Right: *Soda Butte Creek and tailings from the McClaren Mine below Republic Peak.*

Facing page, left: *Spring Creek emerging from the Beartooths.*
Right top: *The Lady of the Lake.*
Bottom: *Elk winter range above Cedar Creek.*

GEORGE ROBBINS

RICK GRAETZ

GEORGE WUERTHNER

ciding whether or not a mine should be allowed. If public costs outweigh public (and private) benefits, a mining proposal could be denied.

The public should get a piece of the action, through royalties from public-owned minerals.

Environmental risk should be properly apportioned. Miners should be responsible for the risk of future environmental costs, such as reclamation.

Such an approval scheme would not deny the Crown Butte mine on its face. If the company could convince the permitting authorities, in consultation with the public, that the project is well enough designed to pose minimal risk to water and other resources, that the site will be better off after reclamation of both old and new mining, that a bond will protect the public in case the company reneges on its obligation, and that the public treasury will benefit, then the mine could be approved. Sen. Baucus, a self-proclaimed friend of both mining and the environment, summed it up: "Mining should proceed only if and when we are absolutely certain that we can protect the integrity of the greater Yellowstone ecosystem."

OIL AND GAS DRILLING

Petroleum geologists have speculated about the possibility of finding oil and gas in the sedimentary rocks that comprise the Beartooth margin of the Bighorn Basin. They believe that the crystalline Beartooth uplift was thrust over older sedimentary rocks, trapping oil and gas below.

In 1985-86, Amoco drilled a well about four miles south of Red Lodge. The well penetrated about 2,500 meters of crystalline rocks in the upper plate of the Beartooth overthrust and about 1,350 meters of sedimentary rocks below. No oil was found.

In the late 1980s, Phillips Petroleum proposed to drill in the Line Creek Plateau. After public outcry, the company opted to drill at a lower elevation on the flank of the plateau. Again, no oil was found. Reclamation of the site was completed, apparently successfully.

In response to the interest in exploring for oil and gas on the north and east flanks of the Beartooth, the U.S. Forest Service prepared an environmental impact statement in the early 1990s. Under the document's preferred alternative, no oil and gas development would be allowed on the Line Creek Plateau. No leases are being approved pending a final decision.

LOGGING

In the 1950s and 1960s, timber harvest in the northern Rockies increased dramatically. Roads and mills were built to match the expansion of the allowable cut by the Forest Service. The result was overexpansion. On a long-term basis, the woods cannot sustain this high level of harvest unless roadless lands are continually opened and the government sells timber below its costs.

As wildlife and wildland resources diminished, public pressure led to the protection of a wilderness legacy—the Absaroka-Beartooth Wilderness. But another legacy was left—a timber industry with real jobs held by real people whose families were an integral part of the local culture.

By the 1990s, each timber sale was controversial. A good example was the Tie Creek sale near Livingston. For years the Forest Service tried to enter this small roadless area over the protests of local citizens and the opposition of professionals within the agency. Finally the sale was dropped from the timber program and Tie Creek was included in the Montana wilderness bill.

The handwriting is on the wall: the Forest Service must return to its roots as a steward of the forests, not a producer of commodities. This agonizing shift could eliminate the commercial timber programs on the Gallatin and Shoshone national forests by the turn of the 21st century.

WATER DEVELOPMENT

The Beartooth Mountains are well known for their high yield of water. Naturally, irrigators and power producers have been attracted to the steep, narrow canyons of the Yellowstone River and its many tributaries. A couple of projects have been built: Montana Power's Mystic Lake hydroelectric installation and the Glacier Lake irrigation dam. Bear Creek, near Gardiner, and the Clarks Fork River near Cooke City once had hydroelectric facilities. In general, however, high construction costs have deterred water development in the Beartooth.

Several times since the 1920s, a dam has been proposed for the canyon of the Yellowstone a few miles south of Livingston. The Yellowstone is the longest free-flowing river in the forty-eight states south of Canada, and Allenspur is the most promising dam site on the river. Project economics have never been favorable and public interest in the blue-ribbon fishery of Paradise Valley has always managed to defend the river successfully. But no dam project can be irreversibly killed. Someday, perhaps during the next energy crisis, the Allenspur phoenix could rise again from the ashes of past battles.

WILDLIFE MANAGEMENT

The Beartooth Mountains are an integral part of the Greater Yellowstone ecosystem—Yellowstone and Grand Teton national parks and millions of surrounding acres of wild, forested lands in the three-state region of Montana, Idaho, and Wyoming. The ecosystem concept stresses that actions in one part of the system affect other elements of the system and the system as a whole. Management of the Beartooth Mountains should take into account the effect of those actions on the Greater Yellowstone ecosystem. Those actions should also be evaluated in the context of the other proposed and ongoing activities. Examples include the complex management of both grizzly bears and elk.

The grizzly is officially classified as threatened, under the Endangered Species Act. In passing the act, and in classifying the grizzly as threatened, our society committed itself to the preservation of biological diversity in general and to the salvation of the grizzly bear in particular.

In the Greater Yellowstone ecosystem, the bear has been in big trouble for many years. In the last decade, its welfare has been variable. The number of cubs is up, but the total population is hovering at 1974 levels, questionably able to maintain its health and genetic diversity over the long term. The bear's survival is dependent on at least two things.

First, its habitat must be protected. Roads, mines, timber sales, ski areas, and other developments cannot continue as though they were happening in isolation. Second, mortality, especially of breeding age females, must be minimized. In particular, human-caused mortality must cease. That means bear–human conflicts must be avoided.

Elk management is as complex and controversial as grizzly management. The principal difference is that the elk population is not threatened. Some argue that elk are too numerous and their range is overgrazed. If so, the long-term prospects for the animal are gloomy and soil erosion resulting from the overgrazing could be reducing water quality in prized trout streams like the Yellowstone River. Elk and trout are important elements of the resource base for a multimillion-dollar hunting, fishing, and tourist industry in Montana and Wyoming. Management of elk, thousands of which summer in the high meadows and subalpine forests of the Absaroka-Beartooth Wilderness, is important to the economy of the region.

OVERUSE

The paradox of formal wilderness designation is that an area must be publicized in order to generate the public support necessary for successful political action. Then, after protection, wilderness recreation is so popular, the very wildness that is protected is threatened by overuse. (Books like this one just make it worse.)

Not long ago, the vastness of the Beartooth provided unsurpassed solitude and wilderness recreation. Now it is one of the *most* popular wildernesses in the country, the most popular one not close to an urban area. On a warm August day, the East Rosebud trail is the scene of a seemingly endless parade. Other popular canyons are almost as busy. Even in the remote nooks and corners, solitude is as fleeting as the falcon.

In response, the Forest Service stocked the wilderness with rangers who educated intrepid hikers in the art of low-impact camping and cajoled the masses to tread lightly on the fragile soils and vegetation.

The results are encouraging. People are littering less and the concept of camps without fires has gained some acceptance. But the root of the problem—too many people—remains. Rationing through a permit system will be the inevitable result of increasing wilderness use.

Even though protected with wilderness designation, the Absaroka-Beartooth faces a variety of threats to its wild integrity. Only eternal vigilance by an informed and involved citizenry at the local, state and national levels can ensure that what we know and love about the Beartooth will endure into the future.

Names on the Map

Absaroka: Many meanings have been attributed to this prominent regional word. Although a precise translation is unavailable, all are meant to capture the essence of its use in the Crow language. Some meanings suggest that the word refers to the Crow people. Several meanings include an avian element, for example the "bird people," "descendants or children of the raven," "children of the large-beaked bird," or "people of the sharp-tailed bird." F.B. Linderman, in his book *American*, claims it was given to the crow by the French voyageurs, who may have gotten it from the Sioux.

The name has been given to a town (Absarokee), a dormitory at Eastern Montana College (Apsaruka), a coal mine (Absaluka) and a mountain range (Absaroka).

Agate Spring: Agates can be found in this spring in the East Fork of Mill Creek.

Arrastra Creek: An old burro gold quartz mill was used here.

Ash Mountain: This prominent mountain near Jardine has the color and appearance of ash.

Bear Creek: A prospecting party in the 1860s encountered a nearly hairless bear cub here.

Beartooth: The name "Bear Tooth" was used as early as 1881 to refer to the range of mountains we now know as the Beartooth. However, the name did not enter common usage till well into the 20th century. Late in the 1800s, the range was most commonly known as the Snow Mountains or Snowy Range. Other names have included the Yellowstone Mountains, the Granite Range (in reference to the high moun-

Above: *Upper Arrow Lake.*
Left: *Beartooth Lake.*

Facing page, top: *Granite Peak.*
Bottom: *Sawtooth Mountain (foreground) and Wolf Mountain (upper right).*

tains around Granite Peak), and the Absaroka Mountains.

The name Beartooth was probably taken from a feature on the landscape, possibly the sharp promontory on the southeast flank of Beartooth Butte, along the Red Lodge-Cooke City Highway. Another possibility is the pointed crag on the east side of Beartooth Mountain, now known as the Bear's Tooth and attributed the Crow name "Na piet say," meaning the same thing. Another theory, this one improbably, names the range after a Crow chief named Bear Tooth who was described in the journal of William Blackmore, an English entrepreneur who accompanied F.V. Hayden to Yellowstone National Park and Cooke City in 1872.

The use of the name Beartooth blossomed when the Beartooth National Forest was carved out of the Yellowstone Forest Preserve in 1908.

Black Canyon: M.E. Martin, a Red Lodge area prospector, named this canyon for the dark dikes exposed there.

Boulder River: The journal of Lt. J.H. Bradley mentioned the Boulder River in 1862.

Buffalo Fork: Bison were common in the meadows of this drainage named in 1883.

Camp Senia: Senia Cronquist was the wife of the proprietor of this camp on Rock Creek, near Red Lodge. The first cabins were built in 1917.

Carbon County: When the county was created in 1909, a committee of its citizens chose the name for the extensive coal deposits in the area.

Chico: The hot springs here were used by the emigrant miners who worked the gravels and veins in 1864. "Chico" was probably a member of a prospecting party led by George Huston, which explored the upper Yellowstone in 1866.

Clark Fork: This fork of the Yellowstone River was named for himself by William Clark when his party passed its mouth in 1806.

Cooke City: Jay Cooke, the Philadelphia financier, was perceived in 1880 as the savior who could deliver this desperate community from its transportation woes. Surely naming the town for him would result in a railroad shortly thereafter...

Corwin Springs: Dr. Fred Corwin owned and developed the hot springs resort and modestly named it for himself.

Daisy Pass: Daisy was the wife of one of the miners at Cooke City.

Davis Creek: The first settler in the West Boulder was Davis.

Dewey Lake, Mount Dewey: The Philippine exploits of Admiral George Dewey were reported to the James Kimball expedition in Cooke City in 1898. Kimball named Mount Dewey for his friend.

Emigrant Peak, Gulch, and townsite: This name refers to the trains of emigrants that entered the territory in 1864. Among their leaders were Bozeman, Bridger, and Coffenbury.

Fishtail Butte: The Fowler brothers, who lived nearby, named this igneous feature for its outline.

Froze-to-Death: Creeks with this name are found in the Boulder valley and between the forks of Rosebud Creek. A tie cutter was found frozen near the stream in the Boulder in 1882.

Gardiner: The town, the Gardner River, and Gardiner's Hole, are all named for Johnston Gardiner, a trapper who lived in the upper Yellowstone for about forty years, beginning in the 1820s.

Hellroaring: One of the most popular names in the Absaroka-Beartooth, Hellroaring has been given to three streams: a tributary to the West Rosebud, a tributary to Rock Creek on the east side of the range, and a major stream flowing south into Yellowstone National Park from the west end of the range. The latter was named by the prospector Hubble in 1867.

Henderson Mountain: A. Bart Henderson was a prospector and adventurer who traveled the Rocky Mountains in the 1860s. One of the discoverers of the New World Mining District around Cooke City, his restlessness moved him on to an unrecorded fate. His mountain namesake is near Cooke City.

Index Peak: See Pilot Peak.

Jardine: A.C. Jardine was the secretary of the Bear Gulch Mining Company when the post office was approved in 1908.

Lake Abundance: Near Cooke City, this is one of the only lakes in the Beartooth Mountains that contains an indigenous population of trout, so many, in fact, that this descriptive title was in order.

Marten Peak: This mountain, one of the few named peaks in the chain that runs south from Livingston, was named by early trappers for the many pine martens seen and trapped on its slopes.

Mill Creek: William Tomlinson erected a saw mill at the mouth of this stream in Paradise Valley in the fall of 1865 to serve the needs of the booming Yellowstone City.

Monument Peak: In 1886, U.S.G.S. surveyors erected a six-foot stone monument on the summit of this mountain near Independence.

Mount Cowen: Sometimes spelled Cowan, this is the highest and most rugged peak in the western part of the Beartooth. According to longtime forest ranger Harry Kaufman, it was named for Secretary of the Interior Cowan. The peak may have been named for George Cowan who was nearly killed by the Nez Perce in Yellowstone National Park in 1878, or for the Cowan family that ranched in Paradise Valley after the turn of the 20th century.

Mount Delano: Secretary of the Interior Columbus Delano, who served under President U.S. Grant, was investigated for fraud in 1875. He, in league with prominent Bozeman businessmen (Nelson Story, to name one), allegedly conned the government and the Indians simultaneously. Delano was found guilty of negligence and incompetence and forced from office; Story became rich.

Mount Douglas: E.M. Douglas was a topographer who mapped part of the Beartooth Range in the late 1880s. In 1889 he reportedly made the first attempt to scale Granite Peak.

Mount Fox: This mountain, north of Cooke City, was named for Dr. J.M. Fox of Red Lodge by James P. Kimball, who explored the area in 1898 and named many peaks. Fox was the manager of the Rocky Fork Coal Company.

Mount Hague: The Kimball party named this peak for Arnold Hague, a geologist who published excellent early work on Yellowstone National Park.

Mount Rae: Rachel Knight and her husband Harry were settlers in the West Boulder around 1884.

Mount Villard: After climbing it, James P. Kimball named this mountain near Granite Peak for Henry Villard, the man who finally got the Northern Pacific Railroad built. Villard, through the Northwest Improvement Company, a Northern Pacific Railroad subsidiary, invested in the Red Lodge coal mines in the late 1890s.

Mount Wilse: Anders Wilse was the young Norwegian photographer who accompanied the 1898 expedition of James P. Kimball to Granite Peak and its surroundings.

Mount Wood: A.B. Wood was with the Kimball expedition in 1898.

Mystic Lake: This West Rosebud lake was called Long Lake until 1918. A Montana Power Company surveyor suggested the new name because of the mystery concerning the lake's depth.

Nye: Jack Nye, a prospector in the Stillwater Complex in the 1880s, convinced the Minnesota Mining and Milling Company to invest in the property, despite questions regarding the true location of the Crow Reservation boundary. The company could have been more cautious; after a $250,000 investment, the development was shut down by the Secretary of the Interior in 1889 when it was found to be three miles inside the reservation.

Pilot Peak: In the Absaroka Range just south of the Beartooth, this prominent peak has guided Indians, trappers, mines, and others to the Cooke City area for centuries.

Tall, pointed Pilot Peak has a shorter neighbor to the northwest, now named Index Peak. Before the 1900s, the names of the two peaks were reversed. The erstwhile Pilot Peak, or Pilot Knob—now Index Peak—was known to the local miners as Dog Turd Peak, an allusion to its profile and a reflection on the vernacular of the profession. The original Index Peak, now Pilot, was named for its resemblance to a sky-directed finger.

Sometime around 1930, the names of the peaks were switched, perhaps due to a mapping error. In any case, the landmark that guides travelers to Cooke City is now known as Pilot Peak.

Red Lodge: Several explanations have been given for the origin of this name; all relate to the Crow Indians, who used the fertile valley of Rock Creek. One is that the Indians painted their lodges with red clay. Another is that the Crow named the place Bad (later mistranslated to Red) Lodge because a supply of meat spoiled and ruined a celebration. Still another is that there were many red man's lodges in the valley.

Rock Creek: Originally dubbed Rocky Fork by early trappers, the U.S.G.S. changed it to Rock Creek.

Rosebud: This name has been applied to the Stillwater River and more recently to a pair of its tributaries. The name comes from wild roses growing near the streams.

Russell Creek: Dave Russell was a buffalo hunter and rancher who settled on the Buck Ranch in 1882.

Shell Mountain: Petrified shells have been found in the sedimentary strata of this mountain southeast of Livingston.

Silver Run Peak and Plateau: A. Lee Corey, the first forest ranger in the east end of the Beartooth, named this peak and plateau in 1896.

Sioux Charley Lake: Settlers called this white man Sioux Charley because he had been adopted by the Sioux as a child. He lived for several years in a cabin at the lake on the Stillwater River named for him.

Slough Creek: "'Twas but a slough," said a miner named Hubble who visited Slough Creek on a prospecting trip in 1867 with Lou Anderson and others, after being impressed with the cascades of Hellroaring Creek, which he also named. Lt. John Slough was lost in the area in 1873 and, fifty years later, was convinced the stream was named for him.

Stillwater: In 1916 Jim Annin penned a beautiful Indian legend describing the Crow legend of the Stillwater. John Bozeman coined the name Stillwater for the sandy ford where the Bozeman Trail crossed the river.

Sundance Lake and Peak: In 1919 a group from Camp Senia carried trout fry to the lake in buckets in hopes of starting a fishery. The sun danced on the ripples of the lake as the fish were deposited.

Whitetail Peak: Legend has it that Ben Greenough shot a whitetail deer on this mountain, completely severing its tail. Anyone familiar with the habitat of whitetail deer and who has seen the long snowfield that stripes the north face of this peak can offer a much more plausible explanation.

Wounded Man Lake: An old trapper and prospector was supposedly wounded by a bear near the lake.

Yellowstone: The entire Beartooth range is in the watershed of the Yellowstone River and partly overlaps the national park. The name was used as early as the 1700s by the French, referring to the yellow rocks along the banks of the lower river. When Lewis and Clark ascended the Missouri River to the Mandan villages in 1805, they heard the name Roche Jaune, or Yellow Rock. Explorer David Thompson used the name in his journal in 1740.

Above: *Island Lake shimmers below Lonesome Point and Castle Mountain.*
Right top: *Lower Arrow Lake.*
Right bottom: *Glacier Lake.*

Facing page, left: *Spring flowers on the Gallatin National Forest.*
Right top: *One of the Rainbow Lakes.*
Bottom: *Hikers pass an unnamed lake above Hollow Top Lake.*

ROB OUTLAW

RICK GRAETZ

PHYLLIS LEFOHN

APPENDIX

ALPINE MAMMALS

All occur in subalpine environments.
(R) = alpine residents
(S) = alpine summer visitors or migrants
From: Pattie, D.L., and N.A.M. Verbeek 1967. "Alpine mammals of the Beartooth Mountains." *Northwest Science* 41(3):110-117.
Scientific names have been updated in accordance with: Wilson, D.B., and D.M. Reeder, eds. 1993. *Mammal Species of the World: A Taxonomic and Geographic Reference*; 2nd ed. Washington, D.C.: Smithsonian Institution Press.

Sorex monticolus Montana shrew (R)
Sorex nanus Dwarf shrew (R)
Sorex palustris Water shrew (R)
Ochotona princeps Pika (R)
Lepus americanus Snowshoe rabbit (S)
Lepus townsendi White-tailed rabbit (R)
Eutamias minimus Least chipmunk (S)
Eutamias umbrinus Uinta chipmunk (S)
Marmota flaviventris Yellow-bellied marmot (R)
Spermophilus lateralis Golden-mantled ground squirrel (S)
Tamiasciurus hudsonicus Red squirrel (S)
Thomomys talpoides Northern pocket gopher (R)
Castor canadensis Beaver (S)
Peromyscus maniculatus Deer mouse (R)
Neotoma cinerea Bushy-tailed wood rat (S)
Clethrionomys gapperi Boreal red-backed vole (S)
Phenacomys intermedius Heather vole (R)
Microtus montanus Montane vole (R)
Microtus longicaudus Longtail vole (S)
Microtus richardsoni Water vole (R)
Zapus princeps Western jumping mouse (S)
Erethizon dorsatum Porcupine (S)
Canis latrans Coyote (S)

Vulpes fulva Red fox (S)
Ursus americanus Black bear (S)
Ursus arctos horribilis Grizzly bear (S)
Martes ameriana Marten (S)
Mustela erminea Short-tailed weasel (R)
Mustela frenata Long-tailed weasel (R)
Taxidea taxus Badger (S)
Cervus elaphus Elk (S)
Odocoileus hemionus Mule deer (S)
Alces alces Moose (S)
Bison bison Bison (S)
Oreamnos americanus Mountain goat (R)
Ovis canadensis Bighorn sheep (R)
Ovis aries (Domestic sheep (S)

ALPINE BIRDS

From: Pattie, D.L., and N.A.M.Verbeek. 1966. "Alpine Birds of the Beartooth Mountains." *The Condor* 68:167-176.

B = alpine breeding birds
R = regular visitors
All others are vagrants.

(F) = Additional species observed by R.S. Fleming on Clay Butte (1973. "Bird communities above tree line, a comparison of temperate and equatorial mountain faunas." Ph.D. dissertation. University of Washington. Seattle, WA).
(H) = Additional species observed by Paul Hendricks and Christopher Norment (1986. "Additions to the alpine avifauna at the Beartooth Mountains." *The Murrelet* 67:90-92).
(H*) = Additional species observed by Paul Hendricks in 1987 and 1988 (personal communication).
(N) = Additional species observed by C.J. Norment (1982. "Avian communities of the alpine tundra/subalpine forest ecotone, Beartooth Mountains, Wyoming." M.S. thesis. Washington State University. Pullman, Washington) near Long Lake and Clay Butte.
Names have been revised in accordance with:

Thirty-eighth supplement to the American Ornithologists' Union checklist of North American birds. Supplement to *The Auk:* 108: 750-754 (1991).

Podiceps nigricollis Eared grebe (H)
Anas crecca Green-winged teal
Anas platyrhynchos Mallard
Anas acuta Northern pintail
Anas clypeata Northern shoveler
Anas strepera Gadwall (H)
Aythya affinis Lesser scaup (H)
Bucephala islandica Barrow's goldeneye (B?) (N) (H)
Circus cyaneus Northern harrier (R)
Accipter striatus Sharp-shinned hawk
Buteo jamaicensis Red-tailed hawk (R)
Buteo regalis Ferruginous hawk
Buteo lagopus Rough-legged hawk (R)
Aquila chryseatos Golden eagle (B)
Falco sparverius American kestrel
Falco columbarius Merlin
Falco peregrinus Peregrine falcon
Falco mexicanus Prairie falcon (B)
Dendragapus obscurus Blue grouse
Charadrius vociferus Killdeer
Tringa solitaria Solitary sandpiper
Actitis macularia Spotted sandpiper (H)
Limosa fedoa Marbled godwit
Calidris bairdii Baird's sandpiper (R)
Gallinago gallinago Common snipe
Larus pipixcan Franklin's gull
Zenaida macroura Mourning dove
Bubo virginianus Great horned owl (R)
Asio otus Long-eared owl
Chordeiles minor Common nighthawk
Aeronautes saxatalis White-throated swift
Selasphorus rufus Rufous hummingbird
Colaptes auratus Northern flicker
Sayornis saya Say's phoebe (B?) (N) (H)
Eremophila alpestris Horned lark (B)
Tachyineta bicolor Tree swallow
Tachycineta thalassina Violet-green swallow
Hirundo pyrrhonota Cliff swallow (B) (N) (H)

Nucifraga columbiana Clark's nutcracker
Corvus corax Common raven (B)
Sitta canadensis Red-breasted nuthatch
Salpinctes obsoletus Rock wren (B)
Cinclus mexicanus American dipper
Regulus calendula Ruby-crowned kinglet (F)
Sialia carrucoides Mountain bluebird (B)
Myadestes townsendi Townsend's solitaire
Turdus migratorius American robin (B)
Anthus rubescens American pipit (B)
Lanius excubitor Northern shrike
Vermovora celata Orange-crowned warbler
Dendroica coronata Yellow-rumped warbler
Oporornis tolmiei MacGillivray's warbler (H)
Wilsonia pusilla Wilson's warbler
Pipilo chlorura Green-tailed towhee
Spizella passerina Chipping sparrow (B)
Spizella pallida Clay-colored sparrow
Spizella breweri Brewer's sparrow
Pooecetes gramineus Vesper sparrow (R)
Passerculus sandwichensis Savannah sparrow (B)
Melospiza lincolnii Lincoln's sparrow (B)
Zonotrichia leucophrys White-crowned sparrow (B)
Junco hyemalis Dark-eyed junco
Agelaius phoeniceus Red-winged blackbird
Sturnella neglecta Western meadowlark
Xanthocephalus xanthocephalus Yellow-headed blackbird
Euphagus cyanocephalus Brewer's blackbird
Quiscalus quiscula Common grackle (H*)
Molothrus ater Brown-headed cowbird
Leucosticte arctoa Rosy finch* (B)
Pinicola enucleator Pine grosbeak (H)
Carpodacus cassinii Cassin's finch
Loxia curvirostra Red crossbill (H)
Cardeulis pinus Pine siskin
Cardeulis tristis American goldfinch

* The American Ornithological Union is considering returning to the previous split: Black rosy finch (*Leucosticte atrata*) and gray-crowned rosy finch (*L. tephrocotis*). The black rosy finch is the Beartooth breeder.

BEARTOOTH ALPINE FLORA
by K.H. Lackschewitz

Following is a list of plants collected in the Beartooth Range of Montana and Wyoming, at or above timberline, from an elevation of about 9,700 feet to over 12,000 feet. Nomenclature, order of listing of families and genera, and common names follow Hitchcock and Cronquist (*Flora of the Pacific Northwest*. Seattle: The University of Washington Press. 1973).

Distribution notation:
*   Arctic-alpine, North American to partly or wholly circumpolar.
Cb Circumboreal.
T   Of lowland origin and appearing more or less often at or below timberline.
W Collected in the Beartooth alpine in Wyoming but not in Montana.
B   Found in Montana only in the Beartooth Mountains.
L   Of limited distribution in Montana and found in the Beartooth alpine.

OPHIOGLOSSACEAE (ADDER'S-TONGUE FAMILY)
Botrychium boreale Milde. Northern grape-fern. T
Botrychium lanceolatum (Gmel.) Angstrom. Lance-leaved grape-fern. T
Botrychium lunaria (L.) Swartz. Moonwort. T
POLYPODIACEAE (COMMON FERN FAMILY)
Cb *Athyrium distentifolium* Tausch (A. Alpestre). Alpine lady-fern.
Cb *Cryptogramma stelleri* (S. Gmel.) Prantl. Steller's rock-brake. Only in limestone.
SELAGINELLACEAE (LESSER CLUBMOSS FAMILY)
Selaginella densa Rydb. var. *scopulorum* (Maxon) Tyron.
Selaginella watsonii Underw. Watson's selaginella. Southern species. L
ISOETACEAE (QUILLWORT FAMILY)
Isoetes bolanderi Engelm. Bolander's quillwort. Dwarf aquatic fern. T

EQUISETACEAE (HORSETAIL FAMILY)
* *Equisetum arvense* L. Common or field horsetail. T
POLYPODIACEAE (COMMON FERN FAMILY)
Cb *Cryptogramma crispa* (L.) R. Br. ex Hook. Parsley-fern. Evergreen.
* *Cystopteris fragilis* (L.) Bernh. Brittle bladder-fern.
* *Polystichum lonchitis* (L.) Roth. Mountain holly-fern. T
Woodsia oregana D.C.Eat. Western woodsia. Usually on slides or in crevices. T
Woodsia scopulina D.C.Eat. Rocky mountain woodsia. Usually on slides or in crevices. T
CUPRESSACEAE (CYPRESS FAMILY)
* *Juniperus communis* L. var. *montana* Ait. Common or mountain juniper. Sometimes above Krummholz.
PINACEAE (PINE FAMILY)
Abies lasiocarpa (Hook.) Nutt. Subalpine fir. T
Picea engelmannii Parry ex Engelm. Engelmann spruce. T
* *Picea glauca* (Moench) Voss. White spruce. T
Pinus albicaulis Engelm. White bark pine. T
SALICACEAE (WILLOW FAMILY)
* *Salix arctica* Pall. Arctic willow. The most common creeping willow in the Beartooth.
* *Salix barrattiana* Hook. Barratt willow. Rare disjunct. L
* *Salix brachycarpa* Nutt. Short-fruited willow. Uncommon.
Salix cascadensis Cockerell. Cascade willow. Rare in Montana and in the Beartooth. L
Salix commutata Bebb. Undergreen willow.
Salix dodgeana Rydb. Dodge willow. Uncommon. West Boulder Plateau on granite.
Salix eastwoodiae Cockerell. Miss Eastwood's willow. Uncommon. T
* *Salix glauca* L. Glaucous willow. Common and often in extensive "thickets."
Salix myrtillifolia Anderss. (*Salix boothii* Dorn). Blueberry or bilberry willow.
* *Salix nivalis* Hook. Creeping snow willow.
* *Salix phylicifolia* L. Tea-leaved willow.
Salix tweedyi (Bebb) Ball. Tweedy's willow. T W and along brooks in deep canyons.

Salix wolfii Bebb. Wolf's willow. T W and at lower elevations of the Beartooth.

BETULACEAE (BIRCH FAMILY)
* *Betula glandulosa* Michx. Bog birch. Widespread, but uncommon at higher elevations. T

POLYGONACEAE (BUCKWHEAT FAMILY)
Eriogonum flavum Nutt. Sulphur flower or yellow buckwheat. T

Eriogonum ovalifolium Nutt. Silver plant or oval-leaf eriogonum.

Eriogonum umbellatum Torr. var. subalpinum (Greene) Jones. Umbrella plant or sulphur eriogonum. T

* *Koenigia islandica* L. Iceland plant. Tiny annual. L B

* *Oxyria digyna* (L.) Hill. Mountain sorrel.

Polygonum bistortoides Pursh. American bistort. Common and very evident for a long season.

Polygonum douglasii Greene. Douglas' knotweed. Annual. T

Polygonum engelmannii Greene. Engelmann's knotweed. Annual. T

Polygonum minimum Wats. Leafy dwarf knotweed. Annual. T

* *Polygonum viviparum* L. Viviparous or alpine bistort.

Cb *Rumex acetosa* L. Garden sorrel. Introduced?

Rumex paucifolius Nutt. Mountain dock or alpine sorrel. T

Cb *Rumex salicifolius* Weinm. var. *montigenitus* Jeps. Narrow-leaved dock. T

PORTULACACEAE (PURSLANE FAMILY)
Claytonia lanceolata Pursh. Springbeauty. T

Claytonia megarhiza (Gray) Parry ex Wats. Alpine spring beauty. Usually on sliderock.

Lewisia pygmaea (Gray) Robins. Alpine lewisia or pygmy bitterroot.

Spraguea umbellata Torr. Pussypaws. Often on disturbed soil around mines.

CARYOPHYLLACEAE (PINK FAMILY)
* *Arenaria capillaris* Poir. Mountain sandwort. T

Arenaria congesta Nutt. var. *congesta*. Ballhead sandwort.

Arenaria congesta Nutt. var. *lithophila* Rydb. Ballhead sandwort.

Arenaria nuttallii Pax. Nuttall's sandwort. Mostly on sliderock.

* *Arenaria obtusiloba* (Rydb.) Fern. Alpine or arctic sandwort. The most common sandwort.

Cb *Arenaria rossii* R.Br. var. *apetala* Maguire. Ross sandwort.

* *Arenaria rubella* (Wahlenb.) J.E. Smith. Reddish or boreal sandwort.

* *Arenaria sajanensis* Schlecht. Pygmy sandwort (a form of A. *obtusilaba*).

* *Cerastium arvense* L. Field chickweed.

* *Cerastium beeringianum* Cham. & Schlecht. Alpine chickweed.

Draba reptans (Lam.) fern. Carolina draba.

* *Lychnis apetala* L. Apetalous campion. Disjunct. Perhaps calcicole. W

* *Sagina saginoides* (L.) Britt. Arctic or alpine pearlwort. Gardeners' "Irish Moss." T

* *Silene acaulis* L. Moss campion.
* *Silene parryi* (Wats.) Hitchc. & Maguire. Parry's silene.
* *Silene repens* Pers. var. *australe* Hitchc. & Maguire. Creeping silene. Uncommon to rare. L
Stellaria americana (Porter ex Robins) Standley. American starwort.
* *Stellaria calycantha* (Ledeb.) Bong. Northern starwort.
* *Stellaria crassifolia* Ehrh. Thick-leaved starwort.
* *Stellaria longipes* Goldie var. *longipes*. Longstalk starwort.
* *Stellaria longipes* Goldie var. *altocaulis* (Hulten) Hitchc. Longstalk starwort.
Cb *Stellaria umbellata* Turcz. ex Kar. & Kir. Umbellate starwort.

RANUNCULACEAE (BUTTERCUP FAMILY)
* *Anemone drummondii* Wats. var. *lithophila* (Rydb.) Hitchc. Drummond's anemone.

Above: On the forest floor.
Left: Lupine.
Far left: Dwarf clover.
Left top: Engelmann spruce.

Facing page, top: Marsh marigold.
Bottom: An unusual orange paintbrush in the Beartooths.

Anemone multifida Poir. var. *tetonensis* (Porter) Hitchc. Pacific anemone.

* *Anemone nuttalliana* DC. Pasqueflower or wild crocus.

* *Anemone parviflora* Michx. Northern anemone. W

Aquilegia flavescens Wats. Yellow columbine. T

Aquilegia jonesii Parry. Limestone columbine. Calcicole on East Boulder Plateau. Endemic in Montana and Wyoming.

Caltha leptosepala DC. Marsh marigold.

Delphinium bicolor Nutt. Low or little larkspur. T

Delphinium glaucescens Rydb. Palish larkspur. Regional endemic, from Park and Deer Lodge counties to Yellowstone and Custer counties. T

* *Ranunculus aquatilis* L. White water-buttercup. T

Ranunculus eschscholtzii Schlecht. Subalpine buttercup. The most common buttercup.

* *Ranunculus gelidus* Kar. & Kir. Arctic buttercup. L B

Ranunculus jovis A. Nels. Jove's buttercup. T L

Cb *Ranunculus natans* Meyer. Floating water-buttercup. T

* *Ranunculus pygmaeus* Wahlenb. Dwarf buttercup.

Ranunculus verecundus Robins. Modest buttercup.

Trollius laxus Salisb. Globeflower. T

PAPAVERACEAE (POPPY FAMILY)

* *Papaver kluanense* D. Love. Alpine poppy. L B

CRUCIFERAE (MUSTARD FAMILY)

Arabis drummondii Gray. Drummond's rockcress. T

Arabis lemmonii Wats. Lemmon's rockcress.

Arabis lyallii Wats. Lyall's rockcress.

Arabis nuttallii Robins. Nuttall's rockcress.

* *Draba aurea* Vahl. Golden draba.

* *Draba crassifolia* R. Graham. Thickleaved draba. Annual.

* *Draba fladnizensis* Wulfen. Austrian whitlow-wort. Disjunct. L

* *Draba glabella* Pursh. Smoothish draba. Disjunct. W L

Draba incerta Pays. Yellowstone draba.

* *Draba lanceolata* Royle. Lance leaved draba.

* *Draba lonchocarpa* Rydb. Snow draba.

Draba oligosperma Hook. Glacier draba.

Draba paysonii Macbr. var. *treleasii* (Schulz) Hitch.

Draba pectinipila Rollins. Comb-hair whitlow-grass. W

Draba porsildii G.A. Mulligan. Porsild's draba. Perhaps northern disjunct. L B

* *Draba stenoloba* Ledeb. Slender draba. Annual.

Draba ventosa Gray. Rare. W L

Erysimum asperum (Nutt.) DC. Plains wallflower or prairie rocket. Biennial; perhaps identical to *E. nivale*.

Erysimum nivale (Greene) Rydb. Alpine wallflower. Perennial; perhaps identical to *E. asperum*.

Lesquerella alpina (Nutt.) Wats. Alpine bladderpod.

* *Parrya nudicaulis* (L.) Regel. Parrya. Perhaps calcicole. Disjunct. W

Physaria saximontana Rollins. var. *dentata*. Mountain twinpod.

Rorippa obtusa (Nutt.) Britt. var. *alpina* (Wats.) Britt. Yellowcress. Along lakes, ponds, and slow-moving streamlets.

* *Smelowskia calycina* (Steph.) C.A. Mey. Alpine or siberian smelowskia.

Thlaspi fendleri Gray. Mountain pennycress or wild candytuft.

Thlaspi parviflorum A. Nels. Small-flowered pennycress.

CRASSULACEAE (STONECROP FAMILY)

Sedum debile Wats. Weak-stemmed stonecrop. Rare. W

Sedum lanceolatum Torr. Lance-leaved stonecrop.

Sedum rhodanthum Gray. Rosecrown. In Montana, common only in the Beartooth. South-central Montana to Arizona.

* *Sedum rosea* (L.) Scop. Roseroot.

SAXIFRAGACEAE (SAXIFRAGE FAMILY)

Heuchera parvifolia Nutt. Small-leaved alumroot. T

Lithophragma bulbifera Rydb. Bulberiferous fringecup.

Mitella pentandra Hook. Alpine mitrewort. T

Parnassia fimbriata Konig. Fringed Grass-of-Parnassus. T

Parnassia kotzebuei Cham. Kotzebue's Grass-of-Parnassus.

Cb *Saxifraga adscendens* L. Wedge-leaf saxifrage.

Saxifraga arguta D. Don. Brook saxifrage. T

* *Saxifraga bronchialis* L. var. *austromontana* (Wieg.) G.N. Jones. Spotted saxifrage.

* *Saxifraga caespitosa* L. Tufted saxifrage.

* *Saxifraga cernua* L. Nodding saxifrage.

Saxifraga chrysantha Gray. Golden saxifrage. A more southern alpine species. L B

Saxifraga debilis Engelmann. Pygmy or weak saxifrage.

* *Saxifraga flagellaris* Willd. Stoloniferous saxifrage. Uncommon disjunct.

Saxifraga hirculus L. Goat saxifrage. L

Saxifraga lyallii Engl. Red-stemmed saxifrage. Eastern Beartooth Mountains. T

Saxifraga occidentalis Wats. Western or redwool saxifrage.

* *Saxifraga oppositifolia* L. Purple saxifrage.

Saxifraga oregana Howell var. *subapetala* (E. Nels.) Hitchc. Bog saxifrage.

Saxifraga rhomboidea Greene. Diamondleaf saxifrage.

Telesonix jamesii (Torr.) Raf. James' saxifrage. West Boulder Plateau.

GROSSULARIACEAE (GOOSEBERRY FAMILY)

Ribes cereum Dougl. Squaw currant. T

Ribes lacustre (Pers.) Poir. Swamp gooseberry. T

Ribes montigenum McClatchie. Mountain gooseberry. T

Ribes setosum Lindl. Missouri gooseberry. T

ROSACEAE (ROSE FAMILY)

* *Dryas octopetala* L. Mountain-avens or white dryas.

Cb *Fragaria virginiana* Duchesne. Wild strawberry. An American boreal. T

* *Geum rossii* (R.Br.) Ser. var. *turbinatum* (Rydb.) Hitchc. Ross' or yellow avens.

Geum triflorum Pursh. Old man's whiskers or prairie smoke. T

Potentilla diversifolia Lehm. Varileaf cinquefoil.

Potentilla concinna Richards. Early cinquefoil. West Boulder Plateau.

* *Potentilla fruticosa* L. Shrubby cinquefoil.

Potentilla glandulosa Lindl. var. *pseudorupestris* (Rydb.) Breit. Gland cinquefoil. T

* *Potentilla nivea* L. Snow cinquefoil.

Potentilla ovina Macoun. Sheep cinquefoil.

Potentilla pensylvanica L. Prairie cinquefoil. T

* *Potentilla uniflora* Ledeb. One-flowered cinquefoil. Disjunct. W

Cb *Rubus idaeus* L. var. *gracilipes* Jones. Wild raspberry.

* *Sibbaldia procumbens* L. Sibbaldia. Common indicator of long-lasting snow cover.

LEGUMINOSAE (PEA FAMILY)

* *Astragalus alpinus* L. Alpine milkvetch.

Astragalus kentrophyta Gray var. *implexus* (Canby) Barneby. Spiny or thistle milkvetch.

Astragalus miser Dougl. var. *hylophilus* (Rydb.) Barneby. Weedy milkvetch.

Astragalus vexilliflexus Sheld. Bent-flowered milkvetch.

Hedysarum sulphurescens Rydb. Yellow sweetvetch.

Lupinus argenteus Pursh. var. *depressus* (Rydb.) Hitchc. Alpine or silvery lupine.

Oxytropis besseyi (Rydb.) Blank. var *argophylla* (Rydb.) Barneby. Bessey's or purple crazyweed. Endemic, southwest Montana and adjacent Idaho.

* *Oxytropsis campestris* (L.) DC. var. *cusickii* (Greenm.) Barneby. Northern or field crazyweed.

Oxytropis lagopus Nutt. var. *atropurpurea* (Rydb.) Barneby. Early or rabbit-foot crazyweed. Endemic in southern Montana and adjacent Idaho.

Oxyropis parryi Gray. Parry's crazyweed. Southwest species, found on limestone mountains, not known in Montana. W

Oxytropis podocarpa Gray. Stalked-pod crazyweed. Perhaps calcicole. Disjunct. W

Oxytropis sericea Nutt. Silky crazyweed.

Cb *Oxytropis viscida* Nutt. Sticky crazyweed. Widespread in the north, Alaska to Quebec.

Trifolium beckwithii Brewer ex Wats. Beckwith's clover.

Trifolium dasyphyllum T. & G. Whip-root clover.

Trifolium haydenii Porter. Hayden's clover. Endemic in south-central and southwestern Montana and adjacent Wyoming.

Trifolium nanum Torr. Dwarf clover.

Trifolium parryi Gray. Parry's clover.

GERANIACEAE (GERANIUM FAMILY)

Geranium viscosissimum F. & M. Sticky geranium. T

LINACEAE (FLAX FAMILY)

Linum perenne L. Blue flax.

CALLITRICHACEAE (WATER-STARWORT FAMILY)

Callitriche heterophylla Pursh. ex Darby. Water-starwort. T

HYPERICACEAE (ST. JOHN'S-WORT FAMILY)

Hypericum formosum H.B.K. var. *nortoniae* (Jones) Hitchc. Western St. John's-wort. East and West Boulder plateaus. T

VIOLACEAE (VIOLET FAMILY)

Viola adunca Sm. var. *bellidifolia* (Greene) Harrington. (Blue) mountain violet.

Viola nuttallii Pursh. (Yellow) prairie violet. T

ONAGRACEAE (EVENING PRIMROSE FAMILY)

* *Epilobium alpinum* L. (Dwarf) alpine fireweed or willow-herb.

* *Epilobium alpinum* L. var. *clavatum* (Trel.) Hitchc. Dwarf fireweed.

* *Epilobium alpinum* L. var. *lactiflorum* (Hausskn.) Hitchc. Dwarf white fireweed.

* *Epilobium alpinum* L. var. *nutans* (Hornem.) Hook. (Dwarf) nodding fireweed.

* *Epilobium angustifolium* L. (Tall) common fireweed. Does not flower in the alpine. T

Epilobium glaberrimum Barbey var. *fastigiatum* (Nutt.) Trel. Smooth willow-herb. T

APIACEAE OR UMBELLIFERAE (PARSLEY FAMILY)

* *Bupleurum americanum* Coult. & Rose. Bupleurum.

Cymopterus bipinnatus Wats. Hayden's cymopterus.

Cymopterus hendersonii (Coult. & Rose) Cronq. Henderson's cymopterus. Southern plant. L

Lomatium cous (Wats.) Coult. & Rose. Common biscuit-root. Widespread.

ERICACEAE (HEATH FAMILY)

Cb *Arctostaphylos uva-ursi* (L.) Spreng Kinnikinnick or bearberry. T

Cassiope mertensiana (Bong.) G. Don (White). Mountain heather.

* *Kalmia microphylla* (Hook.) Heller. (Dwarf) swamp laurel. T

Ledum glandulosum Nutt. Labrador tea.

Phyllodoce empetriformis (Sw.) D. Don Pink or red mountain-heath.

Phyllodoce glanduliflora (Hook.) Cov. Yellow mountain-heath.

Phyllodoce intermedia (Hook.) Camp. Hybrid mountain-heath.

Vaccinium scoparium Leiberg. Whortleberry or grouse-berry. T

PRIMULACEAE (PRIMROSE FAMILY)

* *Androsace lehmanniana* Spreng. Sweet-flowered androsace.

* *Androsace septentrionalis* L. Northern androsace or fairy-candelabra. Annual.

Dodecatheon pulchellum (Raf.) Merrill var. *watsonii* (Tidestr.) Hitchc. Alpine shooting-star.

Douglasia montana Gray. Douglasia.

GENTIANACEAE (GENTIAN FAMILY)

Frasera speciosa Dougl. ex Griseb. Green gentian. T

* *Gentiana algida* Pall. Whitish or striped gentian.

Gentiana calycosa Griseb. Mountain bog gentian.

* *Gentiana prostrata* Haenke. Moss gentian. Annual. Disjunct. L

Gentiana simplex Gray. One-flowered gentian. Annual. T L

* *Gentiana tenella* Rottb. Slender gentian. Annual. Disjunct. L

Cb *Swertia perennis* L. Swertia.

PLANTANGINACEAE (PLANTAIN FAMILY)

Plantago tweedyi Gray. Tweedy's or mountain plantain. T

RUBIACEAE (MADDER FAMILY)

* *Galium boreale* L. Boreal or northern bedstraw. T

VALERIANACEAE (VALERIAN FAMILY)

Valeriana acutiloba Rydb. Downy-fruit valerian.

Valeriana edulis Nutt. Edible valerian.

Cb *Valeriana dioica* L. Northern valerian. T

POLEMONIACEAE (PHLOX FAMILY)

Gilia spicata Nutt. Spicate gilia.

Phlox multiflora A. Nels. Many-flowered phlox. T

Phlox pulvinata (Wherry) Cronq. Alpine cushion phlox.

* *Polemonium pulcherrimum* Hook. Showy or skunk-leaved polemonium.

Polemonium viscosum Nutt. Sky-pilot or sticky polemonium.

HYDROPHYLLACEAE (WATERLEAF FAMILY)

Phacelia hastata Dougl. ex Lehm. var. *alpina* (Rydb.) Cronq. Silverleaf phacelia.

Phacelia sericea (Grah.) Gray. Silky phacelia.

BORAGINACEAE (BORAGE FAMILY)

Cryptantha sobolifera Pays. Miner's candles.

* *Eritrichium nanum* (Vill.) Schrad. Alpine forget-me-not.

Hackelia micrantha (Eastw.) J.L. Gentry. Blue stickseed. T
Mertensia alpina (Torr.) G. Don. Alpine bluebells.
Mertensia ciliata (Torr.) G. Don. Tall mountain bluebells. T
* *Myosotis sylvatica* Hoffm. var. *alpestris* (F.W. Schmidt) Koch.
Mountain forget-me-not.

SCROPHULARIACEAE (FIGWORT FAMILY)

Besseya wyomingensis (A. Nels.) Rydb. Wyoming kittentail
or besseya.
Castilleja nivea Pennell & Ownbey. Snow paintbrush.
Endemic in southern and central Montana and
northern Wyoming. L
Castilleja pulchella Rydb. Showy paintbrush.
Castilleja rhexifolia Rydb. Crimson mountain paint-
brush. T
Mimulus lewisii Pursh. Lewis' or red monkeyflower. T.
Pedicularis bracteosa Benth. Bracted lousewort. T
Pedicularis contorta Benth. Coiled-beak lousewort.

* *Pedicularis cystopteridifolia* Rydb. Fern-
leaved lousewort. Endemic from Madison
County, Montana to northern and
western Wyoming.
* *Pedicularis groenlandica* Retz. Pink
elephant's head. T
* *Pedicularis oederi* Vahl. Oeder's lousewort.
Disjunct. L B
Pedicularis parryi Gray. Parry's lousewort.
Pedicularis pulchella Pennell. Pretty dwarf lousewort.
Regional endemic, Granite County, Montana to
northwestern Wyoming.
Penstemon fruticosus (Pursh) Greene. Shrubby beardtongue. T
Penstemon montanus Greene. Cordroot penstemon.
Mostly on slides.
Penstemon procerus Dougl. Small-flowered penstemon.
* *Veronica wormskjoldii* Roem. & Schult. Alpine speedwell.

CAMPANULACEAE (HAREBELL FAMILY)

Cb *Campanula rotundifolia* L. Scotch harebell.
* *Campanula uniflora* L. Arctic harebell.

COMPOSITAE (ASTER FAMILY)

* *Achillea millefolium* L. ssp. *lanulosa* (Nutt.) Piper var.
alpicola (Rydb.) Garrett. Mountain yarrow.
Agoseris aurantiaca (Hook.) Greene. Orange agoseris.
Agoseris glauca (Pursh) Raf. var. *dasycephala* (T. & G.) Jeps. Pale
agoseris.
Agoseris lackschewitzii Moseley & Hend. Pink agoseris. L
Cb *Antennaria alpina* (L.) Gaertn. Alpine pussy-toes.

Antennaria aromatica Evert. Aromatic everlasting.

Antennaria corymbosa E. Nels. Flat-topped pussy-toes. West Boulder Plateau.

Antennaria dimorpha (Nutt.) T. & G. Low pussy-toes. T

Antennaria lanata (Hook.) Greene. Woody pussy-toes.

Antennaria microphylla Rydb. Rosy pussy-toes.

* *Antennaria monocephala* D.C. One-headed pussy-toes. West Boulder Plateau.

Antennaria umbrinella Rydb. Umber pussy-toes.

Arnica cordifolia Hook. Heart-leaf arnica. T

Arnica cordifolia Hook. var. *pumila* (Rydb.) Maguire. Dwarf alpine heart-leaf arnica

Arnica diversifolia Greene. Sticky arnica.

Arnica fulgens Pursh. Orange arnica.

Arnica latifolia Bong. Mountain arnica.

Arnica latifolia Bong. var. *gracilis* (Rydb.) Cronq.

Arnica longifolia D.C. Eat. Seep-spring arnica.

Arnica mollis Hook. Hairy arnica. T

Arnica rydbergii Greene. Rydberg's or subalpine arnica.

* *Artemisia campestris* L. ssp. *borealis* (Pall.) Hall & Clem. Northern wormwood.

* *Artemisia frigida* Willd. Prairie or fringed sagewort. T

Artemisia michauxiana Bess. Michaux mugwort. T

Artemisia scopulorum Gray. Rocky Mountain sagewort.

Artemisia tridentata Nutt. Big sagebrush. T

Aster alpigenus (T. & G.) Gray var. *haydenii* (Porter) Cronq. Hayden's aster.

Aster foliaceus Lindl. var. *apricus* Gray. Leafy-bract aster.

Aster integrifolius Nutt. Entire-leaved aster. T

Aster occidentalis (Nutt) T. & G. Western mountain aster.

Above: *Douglasia.*
Top: *Alpine forget-me-nots.*
Center: *Bracted lousewort.*
Left: *Saxifrage along South Fork, Wounded Man Creek.*

Facing page, left: *Alpine blossoms.*
Right: *Penstemon.*

* *Aster sibiricus* L. var. *meritus* (A. Nels.) Raup. Siberian or arctic aster.

Chaenactis alpina (Gray) Jones. Alpine chaenactis.

Cirsium hookerianum Nutt. Hooker's thistle, white thistle.

Cirsium scariosum Nutt. Elk thistle.

Cirsium tweedyi (Rydb.) Petr. Tweedy's thistle. Regional endemic, south-central Montana, northwestern Wyoming and adjacent Idaho.

* *Crepis nana* Rich. Dwarf hawksbeard.

* *Erigeron acris* L. var. *debilis* Gray. Northern daisy or fleabane.

Erigeron caespitosus Nutt. Tufted fleabane. Widespread and unusually variable. T

* *Erigeron compositus* Pursh. Dwarf mountain fleabane.

Erigeron eatonii Gray. Eaton's daisy. Absaroka Mountains to T. L

Erigeron flabellifolius Rydb. Fan-leaved daisy. Narrow endemic in Park, Carbon, and Sweet Grass counties and adjacent Wyoming. L

Erigeron formosissimus Greene. Beautiful daisy. Southern Rocky Mountain species. L B

Erigeron gracilis Rydb. Slender fleabane. West Boulder Plateau. Regional endemic, southwestern Montana, northwestern Wyoming and southeastern Idaho. L

* *Erigeron grandiflorus* Hook. W

Erigeron ochroleucus Nutt. var. *scribneri* (Canby) Cronq. Buff fleabane.

Erigeron peregrinus (Pursh) Greene ssp. *callianthemus* var. *scaposus* (T. & G.) Cronq. Peregrine fleabane.

Erigeron peregrinus (Pursh) Greene ssp. *callianthemus* var. *eucallianthemus* Cronq. T

Erigeron radicatus Hook. Taprooted fleabane. L

Erigeron rydbergii Cronq. Rydberg's daisy.

Erigeron simplex Greene. Alpine daisy.

Erigeron ursinus D. C. Eat. Bear fleabane.

Eriophyllum lanatum (Pursh) Forbes var. *integrifolium* (Hook.) Smiley. Oregon sunshine. T

Haplopappus lyallii Gray. Lyall's goldenweed.

Hieracium gracile Hook. Alpine hawkweed. T

Hulsea algida Gray. Alpine hulsea.

Microseris nigrescens Henderson. Black-hairy microseris.

Senecio amplectens Gray var. *holmii* (Greene). Harrington Clasping groundsel. Southwestern species. L B

Senecio canus Hook. Wooly groundsel.

Senecio crassulus Gray. Thick-leaved groundsel. T

Senecio dimorphophyllus Greene var. *paysonii* Barkley. Payson's groundsel.

Senecio cymbalaroides Buek. Alpine meadow butterweed. T

Senecio fremontii T. & G. Dwarf mountain butterweed.

* *Senecio fuscatus* Hayek. Twice-hairy butterweed. Disjunct. L B

Senecio integerrimus Nutt. var. *exaltatus* (Nutt.) Cronq. Western groundsel. T

* *Senecio lugens* Rich. Black-tipped butterweed.

Senecio sphaerocephalus Greene. Mountain-marsh butterweed.

Senecio triangularis Hook. Arrowleaf groundsel. T

Solidago multiradiata Ait. var. *scopulorum* Gray. Northern goldenrod.

* *Taraxacum ceratophorum* (Ledeb.) DC. Horned dandelion.

* *Taraxacum lyratum* (Ledeb.) DC. Dwarf alpine dandelion.

Taraxacum officinale Weber. Common dandelion. Introduced.

Townsendia condensata Eat. Cushion townsendia. L

Townsendia montana Jones. Mountain townsendia. W

Townsendia parryi Eat. Parry's townsendia.

JUNCACEAE (RUSH FAMILY)

* *Juncus biglumis* L. Two-flowered rush. Disjunct. L

* *Juncus castaneus* J.E. Smith. Chestnut rush. Disjunct. L

Juncus drummondii E. Meyer. Drummond's rush.

Juncus ensifolius Wikst. var. *montanus* (Engelm.) Hitchc. Dagger-leaf rush. T

Juncus mertensianus Bong. Merten's rush.

Juncus parryi Engelm. Parry's rush.

* *Juncus triglumis* L. Three-flowered woodrush. Disjunct. L B

* *Luzula parviflora* (Ehrh.) Desv. Small-flowered woodrush.

* *Luzula spicata* (L.) DC. Spiked woodrush.

CYPERACEAE (SEDGE FAMILY)

Carex albonigra Mack. Black- and white-scaled sedge.

* *Carex aquatilis* Wahl. Water sedge.

* *Carex atrata* L. var. *erecta* Boott. Blackened sedge.

* *Carex bipartita* Allioni. Two-parted sedge.

Carex breweri Boott. Brewer's sedge.

* *Carex canescens* Bailey. Gray sedge. T

* *Carex capillaris* L. Hair sedge.

* *Carex capitata* L. Capitate sedge. Disjunct. L

Carex elynoides Holm. Kobresia-like sedge.

Carex geyeri Boott. Elk or Geyer's sedge. T

Carex haydeniana Olney. Hayden's sedge.

Carex illota Bailey. Small-headed sedge.

Carex leporinella Mack. Sierra-hare sedge.

Carex microptera Mack. Small-winged sedge. T

* *Carex misandra* R.Br. Few-flowered sedge. Disjunct. L

* *Carex nardina* Fries. Spikenard sedge.

Carex neurophora Mack. Alpine nerved sedge. L

Cb *Eleocharis pauciflora* (Lightf.) Link. Few-flowered spike-rush.

Cb *Carex nigricans* Retz. Black alpine sedge.

Carex nova Bailey. New sedge.

* *Carex obtusata* Lilj. Blunt sedge.

Carex pachystachya Cham. ex Steud. T

Carex paysonis Clokey. Payson sedge.

Carex petasata Dewey. Liddon's sedge. T

Carex phaeocephala Piper. Dunhead or mountain hare sedge.

Carex praeceptorum Mack. Teachers' sedge. Uncommon.

Cb *Carex pyrenaica* Wahl. Pyrenaean sedge.

Carex raynoldsii Dewey. Raynold's sedge. T

Carex rossii Boott. Ross sedge. T

* *Carex rostrata* Stokes. Beaked sedge. T

* *Carex rupestris* Allioni. Curly sedge.

* *Carex saxatilis* L. Russet sedge. T

* *Carex scirpoidea* Michx. var. *pseudoscirpoidea* (Rydb.) Cronq. Single-spike sedge.

Carex scopulorum Holm. Holm's Rocky Mountain sedge.

Carex spectabilis Dewey. Showy sedge. T

* *Eriophorum callitrix* Cham. Cotton-grass. Disjunct. W
* *Kobresia myosuroides* (Vill.) Fiori. Bellard's kobresia.
Cb *Kobresia macrocarpa* Clokey. Big-head kobresia. W
* *Scirpus cespitosus* L. Tufted clubrush.
GRAMINEAE (GRASS FAMILY)
* *Agropyron caninum* (L.) Beauv. var. *latiglume* (Scribn. & Smith) Hitchc. Broadglumed wheatgrass.
* *Agropyron caninum* (L.) Beauv. var. *unilaterale* (Vasey) Hitchc. Slender wheatgrass. T
Agropyron dasystachyum (Hook.) Scribn. Thick-spiked wheatgrass. T
Agropyron scribneri Vasey. Spreading wheatgrass. T
Agropyron spicatum (Pursh) Scribn. & Smith. Bluebunch wheatgrass. T
Agrostis humilis Vasey. Alpine bentgrass.
Cb *Agrostis scabra* Willd. Winter bentgrass.
Agrostis variabilis Rydb. Variant bentgrass.
Bromus anomalus Rupr. Nodding brome.
* *Bromus inermis* Leys. ssp. *pumpellianus* (Scribn.) Wagnon. Pumpelly brome.
Cb *Calamagrostis canadensis* (Michx.) Beauv. Bluejoint reedgrass. American boreal. T
* *Calamagrostis purpurascens* R.Br. Purple reedgrass. Typical on dry ridge crests.
Danthonia intermedia Vasey. Timber oatgrass.

* *Deschampsia atropurpurea* (Wahl.) Scheele. Mountain hairgrass.
* *Deschampsia cespitosa* (L.) Beauv. Tufted hairgrass.
* *Festuca baffinensis* Polunin. Baffin fescue.
Festuca idahoensis Elmer. Idaho fescue
Festuca idahoensis Elmer. f. *vivipara*. Viviparous fescue. Rare form on the Beartooth Plateau.
* *Festuca ovina* L. var. *brevifolia* (R.Br.) Wats. Alpine fescue.
Festuca ovina L. var. *rydbergii* St. Yves. Rydberg's fescue.
Helictotrichon hookeri (Scribn.) Henard. Spike-oat.
Hesperochloa kingii (Wats.) Rydb. Spike-fescue. T
Cb *Koeleria cristata* Pers. Prairie junegrass. T
Oryzopsis exigua Thurb. Little ricegrass.
* *Phippsia algida* (Soland.) R.Br. Icegrass. Disjunct. Known on the Line Creek, Silver Run, and East Rosebud plateaus. L B
* *Phleum alpinum* L. Alpine or mountain timothy.
* *Poa alpina* L. Alpine bluegrass.
Poa canbyi Scribn. Canby's bluegrass.
Poa cusickii Vasey. Cusick's bluegrass.
Poa cusickii Vasey var. *epilis* (Scribn.) Hitchc. Skyline bluegrass.
Poa fendleriana (Steud.) Vasey. Muttongrass.
Poa glaucifolia Scribn. & Will. Pale-leaf bluegrass.
Poa gracillima Vasey. Slender bluegrass.

Poa grayana Vasey. Gray's bluegrass.
Poa incurva Scribn. & Will. Curly bluegrass.
Poa interior Rydb. Inland bluegrass.
* *Poa leptocoma* Trin. var. *paucispicula* (Scribn. & Merr.) Hitchc. Dwarf bog bluegrass.
Poa lettermanii Vasey. Letterman's bluegrass. Uncommon. Exposed summits.
* *Poa palustris* L. Fowl meadow grass or bluegrass. T
Poa pattersonii Vasey. Patterson's bluegrass.
Poa pratensis L. Kentucky bluegrass.
Poa reflexa Vasey & Scribn. Nodding bluegrass. Common in moist meadows, on north slopes. T
Poa rupicola Nash. Timberline bluegrass.
Poa sandbergii Vasey. Sandberg's bluegrass.
Poa scabrella (Thurb.) Benth. Pine bluegrass.
Sitanion hystrix (Nutt.) Smith Bottlebrush squirreltail. T
Stipa occidentalis Thurb. ex Wats. Western needlegrass. T
* *Trisetum spicatum* (L.) Richter. Spike trisetum.
LILIACEAE (LILY FAMILY)
Allium cernuum Roth. Nodding onion. T
Cb *Allium schoenoprasum* L. Chives.
Erythronium grandiflorum Pursh. Glacier lily. T
* *Lloydia serotina* (L.) Sweet. Alpine lily.
Zigadenus elegans Pursh. Elegant death-camas. American arctic species.

INDEX

Italics indicate illustrations

M.D. COLEMAN

Above: *Island Lake.*
Top right: *Whitetail Peak.*
Right: *Beartooth Falls.*
Facing page: *An Outward Bound group at Sundance Pass heads for Whitetail Peak.*

The Beartooth Range Wildlife
Arrow shows direction of winter migration.

Map by Ed Madej

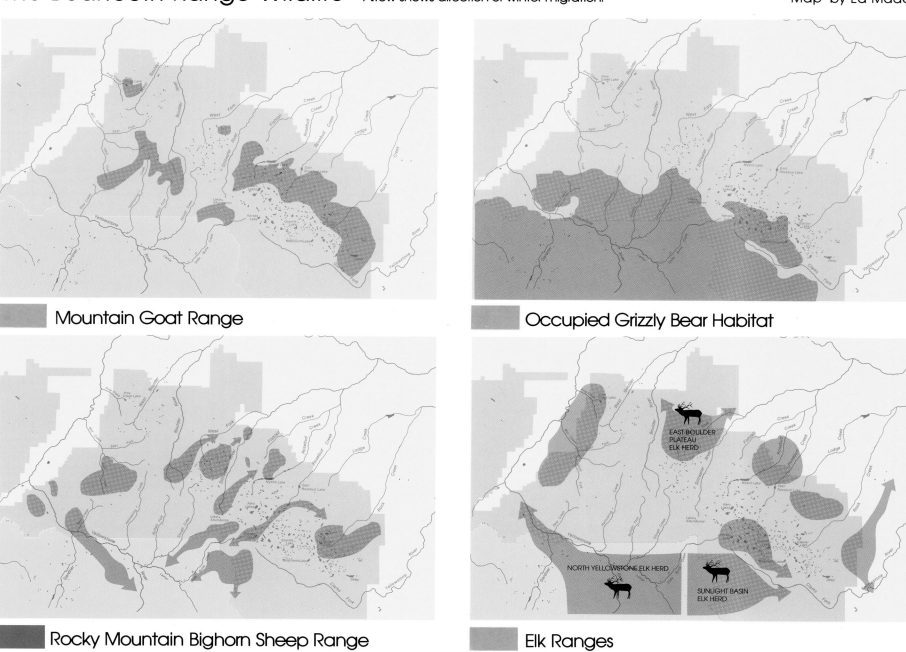

Mountain Goat Range

Occupied Grizzly Bear Habitat

Rocky Mountain Bighorn Sheep Range

Elk Ranges

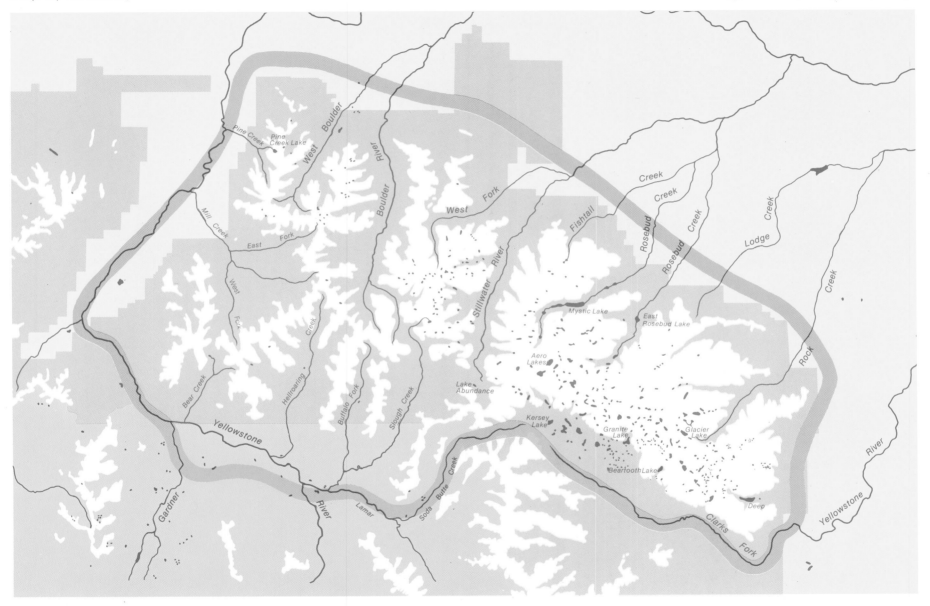

The Beartooth Range Topography

Map by Ed Madej

Land above 9,000 feet in Altitude

Outer Boundary of the Beartooth Mountains

ABOUT THE AUTHOR

Bob Anderson is the chairman of Montana's elected Public Service Commission. A Livingston native and environmental engineer, he was the first board chair and first executive director of the Greater Yellowstone Coalition. As president of the Montana Wilderness Association and the leader of a small group of natural resource professionals called the Absaroka Beartooth Task Force, he played an active role in the political process that created the Absaroka-Beartooth Wilderness.